FTI

SHOW WHAT YOU KNOW® ON THE 3RD GRADE

FCAT

FLORIDA COMPREHENSIVE ASSESSMENT TEST

grade 3

TEST-PREPARATION FOR THE FLORIDA COMPREHENSIVE ASSESSMENT TEST

Show What You Know®
Publishing

NAME _____

W9-AOP-959

Published by:

Show What You Know® Publishing
A Division of Englefield & Associates, Inc.
P.O. Box 341348
Columbus, OH 43234-1348
Phone: 1-877-PASSING (727-7464)
www.showwhatyouknowpublishing.com
www.passthefcat.com

FCAT Item Distribution information was obtained from the Florida Department of Education Web site, August 2007.

Printed in the United States of America
09 08   20 19 18 17 16 15 14 13 12 11 10 9 8 7 6 5 4 3 2

ISBN: 1-59230-288-2

Acknowledgements

Show What You Know® Publishing acknowledges the following for their efforts in making this assessment material available for Florida students, parents, and teachers.

Cindi Englefield, President/Publisher
Eloise Boehm-Sasala, Vice President/Managing Editor
Christine Filippetti, Production Editor
Jill Borish, Production Editor
Jennifer Harney, Editor/Illustrator
Charles V. Jackson, Mathematics Editor
Angela Gorter, Assistant Editor
Trisha Barker, Assistant Editor

About the Contributors

The content of this book was written BY teachers FOR teachers and students and was designed specifically for the Florida Comprehensive Assessment Test (FCAT) for Grade 3 Reading and Mathematics. Contributions to the Reading and Mathematics sections of this book were also made by the educational publishing staff at Show What You Know® Publishing. Dr. Jolie S. Brams, a clinical child and family psychologist, is the contributing author of the Worry Less About Tests and Test-Taking Hints for Test Heroes chapters of this book. Without the contributions of these people, this book would not be possible.

Table of Contents

Introduction

Dear Student:

This *Show What You Know® on the 3rd Grade FCAT, Student Workbook* was created to give you practice for the Florida Comprehensive Assessment Test (FCAT) in Reading and Mathematics.

The first two chapters in this workbook—Worry Less About Tests and Test-Taking Hints for Test Heroes—were written especially for third-grade students. Worry Less About Tests offers advice on how to overcome nervous feelings you may have about tests.

The Test-Taking Hints for Test Heroes chapter includes helpful tips on how to answer questions correctly so you can succeed on the FCAT.

The next two chapters of this Student Workbook will help you prepare for the Reading and Mathematics FCAT.

- The Reading chapter includes a Reading Practice Tutorial, a full-length Reading Assessment, and a Glossary of Reading Terms that will help you show what you know on the FCAT.

- The Mathematics chapter includes a Mathematics Practice Tutorial, a full-length Mathematics Assessment, a Glossary of Mathematics Terms, and a Glossary of Mathematics Illustrations that will help you show what you know on the FCAT.

This Student Workbook will help you become familiar with the look and feel of the FCAT and will provide you with a chance to practice your test-taking skills so you can show what you know.

Good luck on the FCAT!

BLANK PAGE

Worry Less About Tests

Introduction

Many of us get nervous or anxious before taking a test. We want to do our best, and we worry that we might fail. Most third graders have probably heard of the FCAT, although they may not be familiar with the actual FCAT testing situation. Because the FCAT is new to you, you may become scared. You may worry about the test, and this might interfere with your ability to show what you know.

This chapter offers several tips students can use when they face the FCAT as well as many other tests. The ideas will build confidence.

Worry Less About Tests

There are many things most of us would rather do than take a test. What would you rather do? Go to recess? See a movie? Eat a snack? Go swimming? Take a test? Most of us would not choose take a test. This doesn't mean we're afraid of tests. It means we like to do things that are more fun!

Some students do not want to take tests for another reason. They are afraid of tests and are afraid of failing. Even though they are smart enough to do well, they are scared. All of us worry about a test at one time or another. So, if you worry about tests, you are not alone.

When people worry about tests or are scared of tests, they have what is called test stress. You may have heard your parents say, "I'm feeling really stressed today." That means they have worried feelings. These feelings of stress can get in the way of doing your best. When you have test stress, it will be harder to show what you know. This chapter will help you get over your stress and worry less. You won't be scared. You will feel calm, happy, and proud.

If your mind is a mess
Because of terrible stress,
And you feel that you can't change at all.
Just pick up this book,
And take a look,
Our tips won't let you fall!

It's OK to Worry a Little Bit

Most people worry a little bit about something. Worrying isn't always a bad thing. A small amount of worrying is helpful. If you worry about crossing the street, you are more careful. When you worry about your school work, you work hard to do it right. As you can see, a little worrying isn't bad. However, you have to make sure you don't let worrying get in the way of doing your best. Think about crossing the street. If you worry too much, you'll never go anywhere. You can see how worrying too much is not a good thing.

Third graders have a very special job. That job is taking the FCAT. The people who give the FCAT want to know what you're learning in school. FCAT stands for Florida Comprehensive Assessment Test (your teacher may have to explain some of those words), but every time you see the letters FCAT, think to yourself, "**Florida Children Are Terrific!**" All children in Florida are terrific and can learn to do their best on the FCAT without worrying too much or too little.

What Kind of Kid Are You?

Test stress and worrying too much or too little can get in our way. The good news is there are ways we can help ourselves do better on tests. All we have to do is change the way we think about taking tests. You can do better, not by learning more or studying more, but by changing the way you think about things.

Now you will read about some students who need to change the way they think about tests. You may see these students have some of the same feelings you have. You will learn how each of these kids faced their problems and ended up doing better on tests.

Stay-Away Stephanie

Stephanie thought that it was better to stay away from tests than to try at all. She was scared to face tests. She thought, "If I stay home sick, I won't have to take the test. I don't care if I get in trouble, I'm just not going to take the test." Stay-Away Stephanie felt less nervous when she ran away from tests, but she never learned to face her fear. Stephanie's teacher thought Stephanie didn't care about tests or school, but this wasn't true at all. Stay-Away Stephanie really worried about tests. She stayed away instead of trying to face each challenge.

One day, Stephanie's mom had an idea! "Stephanie, do you remember when you were afraid to ride your bike when I took the training wheels off?" her mom asked. "You would hide whenever I wanted to take a bike ride. You said, 'I would rather walk than learn to ride a two-wheel bike.' " Stephanie knew that wasn't true. She did want to learn to ride the bike, but she was scared. She stayed away from the challenge. When Stephanie faced her fear, step by step, she learned to ride her bike. "Stephanie," her mom said, "I think you stay away from tests because you're worried." Stephanie knew her mom was right. She had to face tests step by step.

Stephanie and her teacher came up with a plan. First, Stephanie's teacher gave her two test questions to do in school. For homework, Stephanie did two more questions. When Stephanie was scared, she talked with her mom or her teacher. She didn't stay away. Soon, Stephanie knew how to ask for help, and she took tests without being worried. Now, she has a new nickname; it's "Super Successful Stephanie!"

If you are like Stay-Away Stephanie, talk with your teacher or someone who can help you. Together, you can learn to take tests one step at a time. You will be a super successful student instead of a stay-away student.

Worried Wendy

Wendy always thought that the worst would happen. Her mind worried about everything. "What if I can't answer all the questions? What if I don't do well? My teacher won't like me. My dad will be upset. I will have to study a lot more." Wendy spent her time worrying. Instead, she should learn to do well on tests.

Wendy was so worried her stomach hurt. Wendy's doctor knew she wasn't sick, she was worried. "Wendy," he said, "I have known you ever since you were born. You have always been curious. You wanted to know how everything worked and where everything was. But now, your curious mind is playing tricks on you. You are so worried, you're making yourself sick."

Wendy's doctor put a clock on his desk. "Look at this clock. Is it a good clock or a bad clock?" Wendy had no answer. "Believe it or not, Wendy, we can trick our mind into thinking it is good or it is bad. I'm going to say as many bad things about this clock as fast as I can. First, it's not very big. Also, because the clock is small, I might not read the time on it correctly. Since the clock is so small, I might lose it forever." Wendy agreed it was a bad clock. "But wait," said her doctor, "I think the clock is a neat shape, and I like the colors. I like having it in my office; it tells time well. It didn't cost much, so if I lose it, it isn't a big deal." Wendy realized she could look at tests the way the doctor looked at the clock. We don't have to worry. We can see good things, not bad.

Critical Carlos

Carlos always put himself down. He thought he failed at everything he did. If he got a B+ on his homework, he would say, "I made so many mistakes, I didn't get an A." He never said good things like, "I worked hard. I'm proud of my B+." Carlos didn't do well on tests because he told himself, "I don't do well on anything, especially tests."

Last week, Carlos got a 95% on a test about lakes and rivers. Carlos stared at his paper. He was upset. "What is the matter, Carlos?" His teacher asked, "Is something wrong?" Carlos replied, "I'm stupid, I missed five points. I should have gotten a 100%."

"Carlos, nobody's perfect: not me, not you, not anybody. I think 95 out of 100 is super! It's not perfect, but it is very good. Celebrate, Carlos!" Carlos smiled; he knew his teacher was right. Now Carlos knows he has to feel good about what he does. He isn't sad about his mistakes. He's cheerful, not critical.

Look at the chart below. Use this chart to find out all the good things about yourself. Some examples are given to get you started.

Good Things About Me

1. *I make my grandmother happy when I tell her a joke.*

2. *I taught my dog how to shake hands.*

3. *I can do two somersaults in a row.*

4.

5.

6.

Victim Vince

Vince couldn't take responsibility for himself. He said everything is someone else's fault. "The FCAT is too hard. I won't do well because they made the test too hard. And last night, my little brother made so much noise, I couldn't write my story. It's his fault I won't do well. I asked mom to buy my favorite snack. I have to have it when I study. She forgot to pick it up at the store. I can't study without my snack. It's her fault." Vince complained and complained.

Vince's aunt told him he had to stop blaming everyone for his troubles. "You can make a difference Vince," she said. "When is your next test?" Vince told her he had a spelling test on Friday. "You're going to be the boss of the test. First, let's pick a time to study. How about 4:30 p.m. everyday?" Vince agreed. "Now, how are you going to study?"

"I like to practice writing the words a couple of times. Then, I ask mom or dad to quiz me."

"Great idea. Everyday at 4:30 p.m., you're going to write each word four times. Then, ask one of your parents to review your list. You're the boss of the spelling test Vince because you have a plan."

When Friday came, Vince's whole world changed. Instead of his bad mood and poor grade, Vince felt powerful! He took his spelling test and scored an A–. Vince could not believe his eyes! His teacher was thrilled. Vince soon learned he could control his attitude. Vince is no longer a victim. Instead, he is "Victor Vince."

Vince's Study Plan

TIME	Monday	Tuesday	Wednesday	Thursday	Friday
					Spelling Test!
4:00	Write down spelling words. Then, ask Mom or Dad to help.	Write down spelling words. Then, ask Mom or Dad to help.	Write down spelling words. Then, ask Mom or Dad to help.	Write down spelling words. Then, ask Mom or Dad to help.	
4:30					
5:00					
5:30					
6:00					
7:00	Look at spelling words again.	Look at spelling words again.	Look at spelling words again.	Look at spelling words again.	
7:30					Get a movie for doing well!

Perfect Pat

Pat spent all her time studying. She told herself, "I **should** study more. I **should** write this book report over. I **should** study every minute for the FCAT." Trying hard is fine, but Pat worked so much, she never felt she had done enough. Pat always thought she should be studying. Pat would play with her friends, but she never had a good time. In the middle of kickball or crafts, Pat thought, "I should be studying for the FCAT. I should be writing my book report." When Pat took a test, she worried about each question. "I can't answer this one, I should have studied harder."

"Pat," her principal said, "you have to relax. You're not enjoying school." Pat replied, "I can't do that. There is so much more to learn." The principal gave Pat some tips on how to use her study time better.

- Do not study for long periods of time. Instead, try to work for about 10–20 minutes at a time, and then take a break. Everyone needs a break!

- Ask yourself questions as you go along. After you study a fact, test yourself to see if you remember it. As you read, ask yourself questions about what you are reading. Think about what you are studying!

- Find a special time to study. You may want to think of a good time to study with the help of your parents or teacher. You could choose to study from 4:30 to 5:00 every day after school. After dinner, you could work from 7:30 to 8:00. After you finish studying, do not worry! You have done a lot for a third grader.

- Remember, you are a third-grade kid! School is very important, but playing, having fun, and being with your friends and family is also a very important part of growing up. Having fun does not mean you won't do well in school. It doesn't mean you will do poorly on the FCAT. Having fun in your life makes you a happier person and helps you do better on tests.

"Everyone Else is Better" Edward

Edward worries about everyone else. During holidays, Edward thinks about the presents other people receive. At his baseball game, he worries his teammates will score more runs. Edward always wants to know how his friends do on tests. He spends so much time worrying about what other people are doing, he forgets to pay attention to his own studying.

"Edward, you're not going to succeed if you don't worry about yourself," his grandfather told him. "You need to start talking about what **you** can do. Instead of asking your friend how he did on a test, say, 'I got an 85%. Next time, I want to get a 90%.' " When Edward practiced this, he worried less about tests and was a whole lot happier.

Shaky Sam

Sam was great at sports. He was friendly and funny, and he had many friends. However, Sam had one big problem. Every time he even thought about taking a test, he would start shaking inside. His heart would start pounding like a drum. His stomach would get upset. The night before a test, he started shaking really hard.

Sam's older brother liked to sing. He told Sam he used to get nervous before he sang to a crowd of people. "Sam, we need to trick your body. Don't think about the test, think about something fun and happy."

Sam closed his eyes. He thought about making four shots in a row on the basketball court. He thought about his favorite dessert—vanilla ice cream. He thought about swimming at his neighbor's pool. When he opened his eyes, he wasn't shaking.

Practice thinking happy thoughts, and make believe you are far away from your troubles. Test stress will disappear.

Other Ways That Third Graders Have Stopped Worrying About Tests

Third graders are pretty smart kids. They have a lot of good ideas on getting rid of test stress. This list gives tips on how to stop worrying.

- When I am scared or worried, I talk to my neighbor. She is 70 years old. She is the smartest person I know. We sit on her porch and eat cookies and talk. It makes me feel better to know she had some of the same problems. She did well in school, and I know I can do it, too.
- Everything is harder in third grade, especially reading and math. I didn't want to go to school. I talked to my teacher, and he said, everyday before class we should have a talk. We talk about my homework, and he gives me tips. This really calms me down. When I am calm, I always do better.
- I used to worry that I wasn't doing well in school. I thought everyone else was smarter. My dad gave me a special folder. I keep all my tests in it. When I look at the tests, I see how much I have learned. I know I am doing a good job.

Florida kids are smart kids! You, your teachers, and your family and friends can help you find other ways to beat test stress. You will be surprised how much you know and how well you will do on the FCAT.

Test-Taking Hints for Test Heroes

Introduction

Many third graders have not yet seen a multiple-choice test, such as the FCAT. Before you sit down to take the test, it is a good idea to review problem-solving and test-taking strategies. The words "test-taking strategies" may be overwhelming to third graders, so we have titled the chapter, "Test-Taking Hints for Test Heroes."

This chapter offers several hints you can use when you face the FCAT as well as many other tests. The ideas will build confidence and improve test-taking techniques.

Do Your Best on the FCAT: Think Like a Genius!

Most third graders think the smartest kids do the best on tests. Smart kids may do well on tests, but all kids can do their best. By learning some helpful hints, most kids can do better than they ever thought!

Learning to do well on tests will be helpful to you throughout your whole life, not just in third grade. Kids who are "test smart" feel very good about themselves. They have an "I can do it" feeling about themselves. This feeling helps them succeed in school, in sports, in music. It even helps with making friends. Test smart kids usually do well in their schoolwork too. They believe they can do anything!

Become an Awesome Test Hero!

1. **Fill In the Answer Bubble**
   You will use a pencil to take the FCAT. Think about tests you have taken. To answer questions, you may have written an answer, circled the correct answer, or solved a math problem. The FCAT is different. You will use your pencil to fill in an answer bubble. The test is multiple choice. This means you will have four choices to pick from. After you read the question and all the answer choices, think about which choice is correct. Next to each choice you will see an answer bubble. The answer bubbles are not very big. They are smaller than the end of an eraser, smaller than a dime, and smaller than a jellybean. Even though the answer bubbles are small, they are very important! To answer the question, you must fill in the answer bubble of the correct choice. Only fill in one answer bubble for each question. Fill in the bubble all the way, and do not color outside the bubble. Make sure you fill in the answer bubble neatly when you take the FCAT.

Look at the example below. You can see the correct way to fill in an answer bubble. Practice filling in the answer bubbles in this example.

There was a girl named Devine,
Who thought that a dot was a line!
She didn't fill in the bubble;
She was really in trouble!
When her answers are wrong she will whine!

Correct: ● **Incorrect:**   ● ●

Practice filling in the answer bubbles here: ○ ○ ○ ○ ○

Learning how to fill in answer bubbles takes practice, practice, and more practice! It may not be how you are used to marking the correct answer, but it is one way to give a right answer on the FCAT. Think about Kay!

A stubborn girl named Kay,
Liked to answer questions her own way.
So her marked answer bubbles,
Gave her all sorts of troubles.
Her test scores ruined her day!

2. Only Fill In One Answer Bubble

It is not a good idea to touch the answer bubbles with your pencil until you are ready to fill in the right answer. If you put marks on more than one answer bubble, the people who grade your test won't know which choice you think is right. Sometimes kids get a little worried during the test. They might play with their pencils and tap their answer booklets. This is not a good idea. Look at all the answer choices. Only fill in one answer bubble. This should be the answer bubble for the choice you think is right. Do not put marks in any other answer bubbles.

There was a nice girl named Sue,
Who thought she knew what to do.
She marked all the spots.
Her paper was covered with dots!
And she didn't show all that she knew.

3. Think Good Thoughts

The better you feel about taking tests, the better you will do. Imagine you are a famous sports hero. You feel good about playing your favorite sport. You feel good about yourself. As a sports hero, you don't start a soccer game, football game, baseball game, tennis match, or swimming meet by saying, "This is going to be hard. I can't do it." Instead you say, "This may be a little hard, but I can do it. I am glad I have a chance to do this. I am going to do my best. I know I can." You may think the FCAT is a little hard, but you can do it. When you start the FCAT, remember to think good thoughts. This will help you be the best test hero you can be.

There was a girl named Gail,
Who thought she always would fail.
She said, "Tests are tough,"
"I'm not smart enough."
She had a sad end to her test-taking tale.

4. What Happens if I Don't Do Well on the Test?

The FCAT is one way to find out how much you have learned by the third grade. It is important to try your best on the FCAT, but remember, your friends, parents, and teachers will like you no matter how you do on this test.

> There was a nice boy named Chad,
> Who thought if he failed he was bad.
> His teacher said, "That's not true."
> "I like you no matter how you do."
> Now Chad is glad and not sad.

5. Don't Be Too Scared or Too Calm

Being too scared about tests will get in the way of doing your best. If you are scared, you won't be able to think clearly. If you are scared, your mind can't focus on the test. You think about other things. Your body might start to feel nervous. There is a chapter in this book called "Worry Less About Tests." It will help you feel calmer about tests. Read that chapter so you can feel calmer about the FCAT and other tests.

If you are too calm before taking a test, you might not do well. Sometimes kids say, "I don't care about this!" They might not have pride in their schoolwork. They may be nervous. They may think the FCAT is "no big deal" and may try to forget about it. If you do not think a test is important, and you try to forget about it, you are not thinking good thoughts. Don't be scared of the test, but don't forget about it. You can become a test hero and do your best if you take pride in your work.

> There was a student named Claire,
> Who usually said, "I don't care."
> Her sister named Bess,
> Always felt total stress.
> They weren't a successful pair!

6. Don't Rush, Speeding Through the Test Doesn't Help

The last time you took a test, did you look around the room to see who finished first? If someone handed his or her paper in before you, did you feel like you needed to hurry up? Kids feel that way sometimes, but rushing through questions will not help you on the FCAT. Finishing the FCAT first, or second, or even third is not important. This may be a surprise to learn. Usually, we think speed is good. We hear about the fastest computer, the fastest runner, and the world's fastest train. Speed is exciting to think about, but working fast on the FCAT will not make your test score better. Take your time, and you will be able to show what you know!

There was a third grader named Liz,
Who sped through her test like a whiz.
She thought she should race
At a very fast pace,
But it caused her to mess up her quiz.

7. Read Directions Carefully!

One of the best ways to become a test hero is to read directions. Directions help you understand what you're supposed to do. On the FCAT, it is really important to take your time and to read directions. You may say, "Why should I read directions? I know what to do." Here's a story that may change your mind.

Imagine you are a famous chef. Everyone thinks you make the best cakes in Florida! One day, a group of kings and queens come to Florida for an important visit. They ask you to bake a special cake for them. You have never baked this type of cake before. The kings and queens give you directions, but you don't read them. You think to yourself, "Who has time? I don't need directions. I know how to bake cakes." You don't read the directions and put them in a drawer. This is not a good idea. The directions tell you to bake the special cake at 250 degrees, but you bake the cake at 350 degrees! What do you get? A very crispy cake and very angry kings and queens. You should have read the directions!

Make sure you read directions slowly and repeat them to yourself. You should understand the directions before you begin the test.

There was a nice boy named Fred,
Who ignored almost all that he read.
The directions were easy,
But he said "I don't need these!"
He should have read them instead.

8. Don't Get Stuck on One Question

Some of the questions on the FCAT will be easy. Other questions might be a little harder. Don't let that worry you! If there is a question you're not sure how to answer, use your pencil to put a mark by the question. Remember, mark the question, not the answer choice bubbles. Once you have marked the hard question, move to the next question. When you get to the end of the test, go back and try to answer the hard question. Once you have answered many easy questions, you might be able to answer the hard question with no problem.

If you circle a question and move on, you won't "get stuck." This is a good hint. The FCAT has lots of questions, so you will be able to show what you know. If there is a question that puzzles your mind, just go back to it later.

There was a sweet girl named Von,
Who got stuck and just couldn't go on.
She'd sit there and stare,
But the answer wasn't there.
Before she knew it, all the time was gone.

9. Use What You Know!

By the time you take the FCAT, you will have been in school for four years. You went to kindergarten, first grade, second grade, and now you are in the third grade. You were taught a lot of things in school, but you learned many things in other places, too. You may have gathered information at the library, in a magazine, from TV, from your parents, and from many other places. Third graders have a lot of information in their brains!

Sometimes third graders forget how much they know. You may see a question that your teacher has not talked about. This is OK. You may have heard about it somewhere else. Take a minute to think about all you know.

Let's say you were asked the following question:

Melissa and her family go to California for a vacation. Melissa is excited about going to the beach and to an amusement park. She also really enjoys fresh orange juice. Melissa goes to a store to buy an orange juice treat. The sign says a one-liter bottle of orange juice costs $1.19. If Melissa buys the two-liter bottle, how much orange juice will she get?

Ⓐ a small glass of orange juice
Ⓑ enough orange juice to fill a bathtub
Ⓒ about as much orange juice as in a gallon of milk
Ⓓ enough orange juice to fill a swimming pool

This seems like a hard question. You don't know how much liquid is in a liter. Stop and think for minute! You have heard the word "liter" before, but where? You have seen the word "liter" on plastic soda pop bottles. When you think about the soda pop bottle, it looks about as big as a gallon of milk. Now you know the right answer! Even though you think you forgot the exact size of a liter, you used the information you did remember. You're on your way to becoming a test hero!

There was a boy named Drew,
Who forgot to use what he knew.
He had lots of knowledge.
He could have been in college,
But his correct answers were very few.

10. Luck Isn't Enough!

Have you ever had a lucky number, a lucky color, or even a lucky hat? Everyone believes in luck. A famous football player always wears the same shoes, game after game, because he thinks they give him good luck. This doesn't make any sense. Wearing old, smelly shoes doesn't help him play well. But, he believes in luck anyway. Believing in luck can be fun, but it is not going to help you do well on the FCAT. The best way to do well is PRACTICE! Listening to your teacher, practicing the hints you have learned in this book, and learning every day in the third grade will help you do your best.

There was a cool boy named Chuck,
Who thought taking tests was just luck.
He never prepared.
He said, "I'm not scared."
When his test scores appear, he should duck!

11. Recheck Your Answers

Everyone makes mistakes. Checking your work is very important. There once was a famous magician. He was very good at what he did, but he never checked his work. One night, he was getting ready for a big magic show. There were hundreds of people watching the show. The magician's wife said, "Check your pockets for everything you need." The magician didn't listen. "I've done this a million times," he said to himself. "I don't need to check my pockets." What a bad idea! When he got on stage, he reached his hand into an empty pocket—no magic tricks! Next time, he will recheck his pockets to do the best job possible!

Going back and checking your work is very important. You can read a paragraph over again if there is something that you do not understand or something you forget. In math, you can double check your answers to make sure that they make sense. You will not be wasting time if you recheck your work. It is important to show what you know, not how fast you can go. Making sure you have put down the right answer is a good idea.

A cute third grader named Kath,
Always forgot to recheck her math.
She thought she was done,
But wrote 11 instead of 1!
When her test scores come she won't laugh.

There was a quick girl named Jen,
Who read stuff once and never again.
It would have been nice,
If she reread it twice.
Her scores would have been better then!

Helpful Hints From Other Third-Grade Test Heroes!

Third graders all over the United States have good ideas about tests. Here are some of them!

- Ask yourself, "Did I answer the question that was asked?" Carefully read the question so you can give the right answer.
- Read each answer choice before filling in an answer bubble. Sometimes, you read the first choice, and it seems right. But, when you get to the fourth choice, you realize it is the correct answer. If you had stopped with the first choice, you would have answered the question incorrectly. It is important to read all four choices before answering the question.
- Remember, the FCAT is not trying to trick you! Do not look for trick answers. There will always be a right answer. If the answer choices do not look right, mark the question and go back to it later.
- Don't look around the room! Don't worry about how fast your friends are working, and don't worry about how well they are doing. Only worry about yourself. If you do that, you will do better on the test.

Reading

Introduction

In the Reading section of the 3rd Grade Florida Comprehensive Assessment Test (FCAT), you will be asked questions to test what you have learned so far in school. These questions are based on the reading skills you have been taught in school through the third grade. The questions you will answer are not meant to confuse or trick you but are written so you have the best chance to show what you know.

The *Show What You Know® on the 3rd Grade FCAT, Student Workbook* includes a Reading Practice Tutorial that will help you practice your test-taking skills. Following the Reading Practice Tutorial is a full-length Reading Assessment.

About the FCAT Reading for Grade 3

Reading passages on the 3rd Grade FCAT will consist of approximately 40% nonfiction (informational) and 60% fiction (literary). Acceptable nonfiction texts include: science and history passages, diaries, historical documents, magazine articles, essays, biographies, autobiographies, editorials, advertisements, tables, charts, and graphs.

Acceptable fiction pieces include: short stories, excerpts, poems, historical fiction, fables, plays, and folk tales. Passages may include as many as 700 words and as few as 100. The average number of words per passage is 350.

Item Distribution and Scoring

The 3rd Grade FCAT Reading uses only multiple-choice items.

You will select from four possible answer choices and fill in the correct answer bubble. Although multiple-choice items sometimes ask for the recall of facts, most of the sample items demand a more complex thought process. Each multiple-choice item on the assessment is scored 0 (incorrect) or 1 (correct). Each correct answer adds one point to the total assessment score.

The following chart shows the approximate percent of raw-score points taken from each Reading Content Category.

Reading Content Categories	Points
Words and Phrases in Context	15%–20%
Main Idea, Plot, and Author's Purpose	30%–55%
Comparison & Cause/Effect	20%–45%
Reference & Research	5%–15%

Glossary

alliteration: Repeating the same sound at the beginning of several words in a phrase or sentence. For example, "The bees buzzed in the back of the blue barn."

adjectives: Words that describe nouns.

adverbs: Words that describe verbs.

antonyms: Words that mean the opposite (e.g., *light* is an antonym of *dark*).

audience: The people who read a written piece or hear the piece being read.

author's purpose: The reason an author writes, such as to entertain, to inform, or to persuade.

author's tone: The attitude the writer takes toward an audience, a subject, or a character. Tone is conveyed through the writer's choice of words and details. Examples of tone are *happy, sad, angry, gentle*, etc.

base word (also called root word): The central part of a word that other word parts may be attached to.

biography: A true story about a person's life.

cause: The reason for an action, feeling, or response.

character: A person or an animal in a story, play, or other literary work.

compare: To use examples to show how things are alike.

contrast: To use examples to show how things are different.

details: Many small parts which help to tell a story.

descriptive text: To create a clear picture of a person, place, thing, or idea by using vivid words.

directions: An order or instructions on how to do something or how to act.

draw conclusion: To make a decision or form an opinion after considering the facts from the text.

effect: A result of a cause.

events: Things that happen.

fact: An actual happening or truth.

fiction: A passage that is made up rather than factually true. Examples of fiction are novels and short stories.

format: The way a published piece of writing looks, including the font, legibility, spacing, margins, and white space.

generalize: To come to a broad idea or rule about something after considering particular facts.

genres: Categories of literary and informational works (e.g., biography, mystery, historical fiction, poetry).

Glossary

graphic organizer: Any illustration, chart, table, diagram, map, etc., used to help interpret information about the text.

heading: A word or group of words at the top or front of a piece of writing.

infer: To make a guess based on facts and observations.

inference: An important idea or conclusion drawn from reasoning rather than directly stated in the text.

inform: To give knowledge; to tell.

informational text (also called expository text): Text with the purpose of telling about details, facts, and information that is true (nonfiction). Informational text is found in textbooks, encyclopedias, biographies, and newspaper articles.

literary devices: Techniques used to convey an author's message or voice (e.g., figurative language, similes, metaphors, etc.).

literary text (also called narrative text): Text that describes actions or events, usually written as fiction. Examples are novels and short stories.

main idea: The main reason the passage was written; every passage has a main idea. Usually you can find the main idea in the topic sentence of the paragraph.

metaphor: A comparison between two unlike things without using the words "like" or "as." An example of a metaphor is, "My bedroom is a junkyard!"

mood: The feeling or emotion the reader gets from a piece of writing.

nonfiction: A passage of writing that tells about real people, events, and places without changing any facts. Examples of nonfiction are an autobiography, a biography, an essay, a newspaper article, a magazine article, a personal diary, and a letter.

onomatopoeia: The use of words in which the sound of the word suggests the sound associated with it. For example, buzz, hiss, splat.

opinion: What one thinks about something or somebody; an opinion is not necessarily based on facts. Feelings and experiences usually help a person form an opinion.

passage: A passage or writing that may be fiction (literary/narrative) or nonfiction (informational/expository).

persuade: To cause to do something by using reason or argument; to cause to believe something.

plan: A method of doing something that has been thought out ahead of time.

plot: A series of events that make up a story. Plot tells "what happens" in a story, novel, or narrative poem.

plot sequence: The order of events in a story.

poetry: A type of writing that uses images and patterns to express feelings.

Glossary

point of view: The way a story is told; it could be in first person, omniscient, or in third person.

predict: The ability of the reader to know or expect that something is going to happen in a text before it does.

prefix: A group of letters added to the beginning of a word. For example, <u>un</u>tie, <u>re</u>build, <u>pre</u>teen.

preposition: A word that links another word or group of words to other parts of the sentence. Examples are *in, on, of, at, by, between, outside*, etc.

problem: An issue or question in a text that needs to be answered.

published work: The final writing draft shared with the audience.

reliable: Sources used for writing that are trustworthy.

resource: A source of help or support.

rhyme: When words have the same last sound. For example, hat/cat, most/toast, ball/call.

root word (also called base word): The central part of a word that other word parts may be attached to.

schema: The accumulated knowledge that a person can draw from life experiences to help understand concepts, roles, emotions, and events.

sentence: A group of words that express a complete thought. It has a subject and a verb.

sequential order: The arrangement or ordering of information, content, or ideas (e.g., a story told in chronological order describes what happened first, then second, then third, etc.).

setting: The time and place of a story or play. The setting helps to create the mood in a story, such as inside a spooky house or inside a shopping mall during the holidays.

simile: A comparison between two unlike things, using the words "like" or "as." "Her eyes are as big as saucers" is an example of a simile.

solution: An answer to a problem.

stanzas: Lines of poetry grouped together.

story: An account of something that happened.

story elements: The important parts of the story, including characters, setting, plot, problem, and solution.

style: A way of writing that is individual to the writer, such as the writer's choice of words, phrases, and images.

suffix: A group of letters added to the end of a word. For example, teach<u>er</u>, color<u>ful</u>, sugar<u>less</u>, etc.

summary: To retell what happens in a story in a short way by telling the main ideas, not details.

Glossary

supporting details: Statements that often follow the main idea. Supporting details give you more information about the main idea.

symbolism: Something that represents something else. For example, a dove is a symbol for peace.

synonyms: Words with the same, or almost the same, meaning (e.g., *sketch* is a synonym of *draw*).

theme: The major idea or topic that the author reveals in a literary work. A theme is usually not stated directly in the work. Instead, the reader has to think about all the details of the work and then make an inference (an educated guess) about what they all mean.

title: A name of a book, film, play, piece of music, or other work of art.

tone: A way of writing that conveys a feeling.

topic sentence: A sentence that states the main idea of the paragraph.

valid: Correct, acceptable.

verb: A word that shows action or being.

voice: To express a choice or opinion.

Reading Practice Tutorial

Directions for Taking the Reading Practice Tutorial

The Reading Practice Tutorial contains eight reading passages and 20 practice questions. It should take about 30 to 45 minutes to read the passages and answer all the questions. You will mark your answers in this workbook. If you don't understand a question, just ask your teacher to explain it to you.

This section will review the Strands, Standards, and Benchmarks used to assess student achievement in the state of Florida. Following the description of each Benchmark, a sample reading passage and practice items are given. Each item gives you an idea of how the Benchmark may be assessed. Review these items to increase your familiarity with FCAT-style multiple-choice questions. Once you have read through this Tutorial section, you will be ready to complete the Reading Assessment.

Tips for Taking the FCAT Reading

Here are some hints to help you show what you know when you take the Reading Practice Tutorial and the Reading Assessment:

- Read the directions carefully. Ask your teacher to explain any directions you do not understand.

- Read the passages and questions very carefully. You may look back at a passage as often as you like.

- Answer the questions you are sure about first. If a question seems too difficult, skip it and go back to it later.

- Be sure to fill in the answer bubbles correctly. Do not make any stray marks around answer spaces.

- Think positively. Some questions may seem hard, but others will be easy.

- Check each answer to make sure it is the best answer for the question asked.

- Relax. Some people get nervous about tests. It's natural. Just do your best.

Sample Multiple-Choice Item

To help you understand how to answer the test questions, look at the sample test question below. It is included to show you what a multiple-choice question in the test is like and how to mark your answer in your workbook.

1 What is the main reason the author includes a letter written to Robert?

   Ⓐ   to help us understand why Robert wanted to visit his grandfather

   ●   to prove that Robert's grandfather was alive

   Ⓒ   to make us feel for Robert's grandfather

   Ⓓ   to tell us what he thinks about Robert's grandfather

For this sample question, the correct answer is Choice B "to prove that Robert's grandfather was alive"; therefore, the circle next to Choice B is filled in.

Reading Practice Tutorial

Read the poem "Clouds" before answering Numbers 1 through 3.

Look up at the clouds
And what do you see?

I see a man's face
Looking back at me.

He has two big eyes,
A nose, and an ear.

I wonder now
If clouds need to hear.

Gray but glowing
Like the man on the moon.

I know it's not him.
It's just after noon.

Puffy like pillows
Clouds creep on their own,

Sneaking away slowly
To places unknown.

But then the cloud changes
As I watch from below.

The face fades away
And leaves only a glow.

Now answer Numbers 1 through 3. Base your answers on the poem "Clouds."

1 Read this sentence from the poem.

> **The face fades away.**

When the face *fades*, it

Ⓐ   slowly disappears.

Ⓑ   gets bigger.

Ⓒ   moves in circles.

Ⓓ   changes color.

2 Read these lines from the poem.

> **Sneaking away slowly**
> **To places unknown.**

What is the meaning of the prefix *un–*?

Ⓕ   before

Ⓖ   two

Ⓗ   again

Ⓘ   not

3 Which word from the poem tells how the cloud moves?

Ⓐ   wonder

Ⓑ   puffy

Ⓒ   quickly

Ⓓ   sneaking

Read the article "Marsupials" before answering Numbers 4 through 6.

What are Marsupials?

The word marsupial means "pouched animal." Marsupials are mammals. They are warm-blooded animals. They are born live, and they drink their mothers' milk. There is something special about marsupials: they have a pouch. The female marsupial's pouch is like a built-in nursery. Soon after its birth, a baby marsupial finds its way to its mother's pouch. A baby marsupial will live and grow in the pouch for several months.

Most marsupials live in Australia. Australia is a continent in the South Pacific Ocean. There are about 200 types of marsupials in the world. Types of marsupials include kangaroos, koalas, wombats, Tasmanian devils, wallabies, and opossums. The opossum is the only marsupial that lives in North America.

KANGAROOS

Facts about Kangaroos

Kangaroos usually come to mind when people think of pouched animals. There are many types of kangaroos, including the red, the rat, and the gray. Kangaroos grow to many sizes. Some are only one foot tall, but others grow to be six feet high. Kangaroos never run. Their back legs would get in the way if they tried. Instead, kangaroos use their long, strong back legs to help them jump up to three or four times their body's length. They also push off the ground with their tails as they begin a jump. Although kangaroos can jump at speeds of up to 30 miles per hour, they can only hop at this speed for very short distances.

Go On ▶

Kangaroos live in groups called mobs. A mob may include 100 kangaroos. If you want to see a kangaroo, your best chance would be at night or very early in the morning when they are most active. During the middle of the day, they try to stay cool under trees or bushes. They live in many different settings (places) including grasslands, hills, or woodlands. Kangaroos like to graze on grass and other small plants.

Kangaroo Babies

Baby kangaroos weigh about one ounce at birth. They are about the size of a lima bean. They are blind at birth and have no fur. A baby kangaroo lives in its mother's pouch for about five months. Baby kangaroos are called joeys, but they are also known as "young-at-foot." Kangaroos usually give birth to only one baby at the time, but kangaroo mothers with "twins" have been spotted.

Facts about Koalas

The koala looks like a teddy bear, but it is not a bear at all. In fact, koalas may be more like monkeys. They live in trees, and they use their strong claws to hold on to branches in eucalyptus trees.

Koalas must live in thick eucalyptus forests, because adults need to eat between one and two pounds of the leaves daily. Koalas rarely drink water. They get the water they need from the leaves of the eucalyptus tree. The word "koala" actually means "no drink."

Baby Koalas

Koalas are one of the types of marsupials whose pouches open to the rear of their bodies. A baby koala lives in its mother's pouch for seven months. Then, the baby moves to the mother's back and lives in this "piggyback" position for five more months.

Now answer Numbers 4 through 6. Base your answers on the article "Marsupials."

4 Which sentence BEST describes the main idea of "Marsupials"?

Ⓕ Koalas are like teddy bears.

Ⓖ Kangaroos and koalas are two types of marsupials living in Australia.

Ⓗ The opossum is the only marsupial that lives in North America.

Ⓘ Baby kangaroos weigh only one ounce at birth.

5 Which fact about kangaroos is NOT in the article?

Ⓐ Kangaroos are excellent swimmers.

Ⓑ Kangaroos eat grass and other small plants.

Ⓒ Kangaroos can jump at speeds up to 30 miles per hour.

Ⓓ Kangaroos are most active at night and early morning.

6 What topic is this article about?

Ⓕ mammals

Ⓖ kangaroos

Ⓗ pouched animals

Ⓘ koalas

Read the story "The Kitchen" before answering Numbers 7 through 8.

My favorite room in the house is the kitchen. I love to eat, so that's my number one reason. But there are other reasons, too. I love the yummy smells that come from the oven when a cake or cookies are baking. I love the way the kitchen sounds: bacon sizzling in a frying pan, or the kettle whistling on the stove. I love squishing ground beef in my fingers and forming the perfect size hamburger. I love to see foods changing shape as they cook on the stove or in the oven. And the tastes! Just think of juicy lemons, oatmeal cookies, cheesy pizza, warm biscuits, crisp apples, and fresh tomatoes. My list of favorites goes on and on. I think I'll head to the kitchen now. For some reason, my stomach is growling.

Now answer Numbers 7 through 8. Base your answers on the story "The Kitchen."

7 Why did the author write this story?

Ⓐ   to tell the reader how to cook

Ⓑ   to describe the author's favorite room

Ⓒ   to persuade the reader to choose the kitchen as his or her favorite room

Ⓓ   to tell the reader how much the author likes to eat

8 Which words describe something the author feels?

Ⓕ   cookies baking

Ⓖ   bacon sizzling

Ⓗ   squishing ground beef

Ⓘ   pizza baking

Read the article "Frogs and Toads" before answering Numbers 9 through 11.

The Harrison Elementary Press
A Newspaper Written By Kids, For Kids

March Issue	Science Section, Page 1

FROGS AND TOADS
By Federico Garcia

It's important to look to see if the animal you are about to kiss is a frog or a toad. You may never find a handsome prince if you kiss the wrong amphibian. Can you tell the difference between a frog and a toad?

It is easy to confuse frogs and toads just by looking at them. They are both amphibians. This means they can live both in water and on land. They both are coldblooded. This means their body temperatures are the same as the air temperatures around them. They have to look for cool, shady places to rest if they become too hot. Frogs and toads look for warm, sunny places if they are too cold. Both animals are vertebrates. This means they have spines. Their body shape is almost the same. Their eyes protrude out from their faces, so they can see in most directions without turning their heads.

Frogs and toads use their long, sticky tongues to catch insects to eat. Both frogs and toads swallow their food whole.

How are frogs and toads different? Frogs are better swimmers and jumpers because they have long back legs. A toad's back legs are shorter. Frogs are more likely to be found near water. Toads often live in drier places. Most frogs have four webbed feet. Toads do not have webs on their back feet. The skin of a frog is smooth and damp. Toads have drier skin that is covered with bumps called glands. Frogs have teeth in their upper jaws and no teeth in their lower jaws. Toads have no teeth at all.

As you can see, frogs and toads are not the same type of amphibian. Of course, a frog turning into a handsome prince only happens in fairy tales. Who would kiss a frog or a toad anyway?

Now answer Numbers 9 through 11. Base your answers on the article "Frogs and Toads."

9 How are frogs and toads DIFFERENT?

   Ⓐ   their tongues

   Ⓑ   their body shape

   Ⓒ   their eyes

   Ⓓ   their skin

10 Which BEST describes both frogs and toads?

   Ⓕ   coldblooded

   Ⓖ   damp skin

   Ⓗ   four webbed feet

   Ⓘ   long back legs

11 Are frogs and toads BOTH vertebrates?

   Ⓐ   Yes, because both animals have backbones.

   Ⓑ   Yes, because both animals can swim.

   Ⓒ   No, because only frogs are vertebrates.

   Ⓓ   No, because they are both amphibians.

Go On

Read the article "Georgia" and look over the map of Georgia before answering Numbers 12 through 13.

Georgia

Georgia was founded as a colony by James Oglethorpe in 1733. A colony is made up of a group of people who live together in a certain area. Georgia was named in honor of King George II of Great Britain. The first city in Georgia was Savannah. It was settled the same year the colony was formed. In 1788, Georgia became the fourth state in the United States of America. At that time, Georgia's population was around 60,000 people. Today, Georgia is home to more than 8 million people. Georgia is often called "The Peach State." Its capital city is Atlanta.

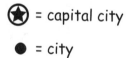 ★ = capital city

● = city

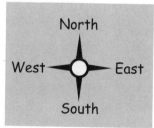

Go On ▶

Now answer Numbers 12 through 13. Base your answers on the article "Georgia" and the map of Georgia.

12 What is the capital of Georgia?

    Ⓕ   The Peach State

    Ⓖ   Atlanta

    Ⓗ   Savannah

    Ⓘ   Oglethorpe

13 Which state does NOT border Georgia?

    Ⓐ   Florida

    Ⓑ   Tennessee

    Ⓒ   South Carolina

    Ⓓ   New York

Go On

Read the story "Hiccup Man" before answering Numbers 14 through 15.

Have you heard the story of Dan, The Hiccup Man? In third grade, Dan was the shortest kid in class. He couldn't reach the top library shelf or the coat rack. When he stood behind his classmates, he couldn't see anything. Dan wouldn't play basketball because he thought he was too short. There was something Dan didn't know: a few hiccups were about to change everything.

One hot, dry, summer day, Dan was on his way to dance class. He stopped to get a cold drink. He was so thirsty, he felt like he was going to dry up and blow away. Dan got a cold soda from a vending machine on the corner. He drank it so fast, he could hardly taste the cola flavor. He stopped and looked at the can for a second. That's when the hiccups started.

The hiccups weren't so bad, at first. In fact, it was his best dance practice ever. The hiccups seemed to help him jump higher, twirl faster, and dance better. Everyone in the class wanted to know what he had done to improve so much. Dan could only hiccup and smile. He didn't have an answer.

He put on his jeans and T-shirt after class. "That's strange," he thought to himself as he buttoned his pants. "These feel tight." He tied his shoes and started toward home. Dan hiccuped with every other step. By the time he got home, his pants seemed four inches short. His T-shirt was so tight, he couldn't wait to change. And to make things worse, Dan's sides hurt from all his hiccuping.

He tried everything he knew to make the hiccups stop. He held his breath. No hiccups…no hiccups…no…HIC! That didn't work. He looked for someone to scare him. He found his brother in the kitchen, but his brother started laughing. Dan's toes were sticking out of his sneakers. Dan had grown far too big for his clothes. With all his giggling, Dan's brother couldn't scare anyone. Dan tried a spoonful of sugar but hiccuped just as he got the spoon to his mouth. The sugar spilled all over the floor.

Dan's hiccups went on and on. The more he hiccuped, the taller he grew. Dan worried the hiccups would never end, but then suddenly one morning, they stopped. Something else happened, too. Dan stopped growing. Dan was so tired from all that hiccuping and growing, he slept for a week. He woke up just in time for school to start.

Dan was excited about his new height. On the first day of school, his friends barely recognized him. He was the tallest kid in school! When his teacher asked Dan what he did over summer vacation, he smiled and said, "I hiccuped." The kids laughed and started calling him Dan, Dan the Hiccup Man. Dan said he didn't mind, as long the hiccups never came back.

Go On

40 Student Workbook

Now answer Numbers 14 through 15. Base your answers on the story "Hiccup Man."

14 What was Dan's BIGGEST problem?

    Ⓕ   Dan's classmates called him the Hiccup Man.

    Ⓖ   Dan was the worst dancer in his class.

    Ⓗ   Dan couldn't stop hiccuping.

    Ⓘ   Dan couldn't play basketball.

15 How was Dan's problem solved?

    Ⓐ   Dan takes a special medicine.

    Ⓑ   No reason is given.

    Ⓒ   Dan goes to the doctor.

    Ⓓ   Dan dances until his problem is solved.

Read the story "Birds of a Feather" before answering Numbers 16 through 18.

Spring arrived and, as always, the race was on. Who would have the biggest, the best built, and the most attractive nests this year? It was the only thing the birds of the neighborhood could think about.

Mrs. Sparrow and Mrs. Jay were having a snack at the local bird feeder. "Have you talked to the new neighbors yet?" Mrs. Sparrow asked.

"No, I haven't, but I can see they've been busy. Have you seen the nest they're building? It's beautiful," Mrs. Jay replied.

"Yes, it seems to be quite a nest for a newcomer. I wonder where they got the idea. I've never seen a bird who could weave grasses together in the way they have."

Mrs. Jay wiped a bit of birdseed from her beak before she answered. "They do seem to be talented. I've been watching, since they are so close to my nest. Their nest will probably be the biggest one in our neighborhood. But I'm quite comfortable in our nest. My husband, Blue, did a wonderful job finding just the right blend of grasses, sticks, bark, and feathers for our nest this year. It may not be the largest, but it is just right for our family. I'm very proud of our home."

"As you should be. It does look quite cozy. Do you remember two years ago when the Hummingbird family made their nest here? It was so tiny, even smaller than my home."

Go On ▶

42   Student Workbook

"That's true," Mrs. Jay chirped. "They were always humming while they worked. I wondered if they had forgotten the words to their songs."

Mrs. Sparrow laughed. "No, no, no. The humming came from their wings moving so rapidly. But I never found them to be very friendly. And the Robins! They're not so nice! Just because they have those beautiful, red breast feathers doesn't mean they can be unfriendly. I mean, look at the Cardinals. They have beautiful red feathers, too, but you don't see them flying away every time another bird comes by the feeder. Besides I think we're all beautiful in our own ways. Don't you?"

"Yes, I do agree with you. Oh, no! The people in the yellow house just let their dog out. Once he sees us, we won't be able to hear ourselves chirp. I think I'll head back to my nest rather than listen to him. I'll see you later, Mrs. Sparrow." Mrs. Jay tweeted her goodbye and flew away.

Mrs. Sparrow ate another seed before she heard the barking begin. "There goes the neighborhood," she thought to herself and flew toward her home.

Now answer Numbers 16 through 18. Base your answers on the story "Birds of a Feather."

16 How are Mrs. Jay's nest and the new birds' nest DIFFERENT?

  (F) Mrs. Jay's nest is smaller than the new birds' nest.

  (G) Mrs. Jay's nest is larger than the new birds' nest.

  (H) Mrs. Jay's nest is built with the best materials.

  (I) Mrs. Jay's nest is more beautiful than the new birds' nest.

17 Mrs. Jay and Mrs. Sparrow like which family of birds BEST?

  (A) the Robins

  (B) the Cardinals

  (C) the Hummingbirds

  (D) the Wrens

18 How are Mrs. Jay and Mrs. Sparrow ALIKE?

  (F) They both like the dog in the yellow house.

  (G) They made their nests in the same tree.

  (H) They both dislike the dog in the yellow house.

  (I) They both dislike eating at the bird feeder.

Go On

Read the story "The Upset Storm" before answering Numbers 19 through 20.

The Upset Storm

I had waited for this day for weeks. The day of our big field trip had arrived, finally, the fun trip. This wasn't a trip to a museum or a play. We weren't going to listen to someone talk about desert plants. This trip was about having fun. My classmates and I would soon be riding water slides and splashing in the big pool's blue waters. I couldn't wait.

Mom packed my lunch. My juice box was at the bottom of the bag. My sandwich and chips were on the top so they wouldn't get smashed. I knew what I wanted to wear. I put my new T-shirt, my swimsuit, and a big towel on a chair in my room. I set two alarm clocks. I didn't want to oversleep. I wanted everything to be perfect.

Before I went to sleep, I watched the TV weatherman. He said a big storm was coming. I changed the channel. I hoped a new weather report would be different. It was not. A big storm would arrive the next morning, the morning of our big day, the day of the fun trip.

I thought about the trip. I couldn't sleep. Up in my room, I hoped for better weather. But I knew the storm was going to upset our plans. I couldn't believe it. A storm! Instead of splashing in the pool, I would be sitting at my desk, working on math problems. How could the weather do this to me?

Now answer Numbers 19 through 20. Base your answers on the story "The Upset Storm."

19 How will the storm affect the field trip?

(A)   The class will go on a different field trip.

(B)   The field trip will be rescheduled for another day.

(C)   The field trip will not be affected by the storm.

(D)   The field trip will be cancelled.

20 Why did the author watch weather forecasts on different channels?

(F)   She hoped they would all forecast a storm.

(G)   She hoped the weather forecast might be different on another channel.

(H)   She didn't have anything else to do.

(I)   She wanted to know what the weather would be like the next week.

This is the end of the Reading Practice Tutorial.
Until time is called, go back and check your work or answer questions
you did not complete. When you have finished, close your workbook.

Reading Assessment

Directions for Taking the Reading Assessment

This Assessment test contains eight reading passages and 50 questions. Some of the passages are fiction, while others are nonfiction. Read each passage and the questions that follow carefully. You may look back at any passage as many times as you would like. If you are unsure of a question, you can move to the next question, and go back to the question you skipped later.

This test contains multiple-choice questions. Multiple-choice questions require you to pick the best answer out of four possible choices. Only one answer is correct. Remember to read the questions and the answer choices carefully. You will mark your answers in this workbook. Fill in the answer bubble to mark your selection.

Reading Assessment

Read the article "A Symbol of Pride" and look over the fact box "The America Flag" before answering Numbers 1 though 6.

An important patriotic symbol of the United States is our national flag. Our flag represents the land, the people, and the government of the United States. On June 14, 1777, the Continental Congress declared (said) the flag of the United States would have thirteen stripes. The stripes would alternate red and white. This means one stripe would be red, the next stripe would be white; then, the next stripe would be red, and so on. The Continental Congress also said the flag would have a union (group) of thirteen white stars on a blue background. The thirteen stripes represented the thirteen original colonies. These thirteen colonies were the first states in the United States. The thirteen stars represented the number of states in the United States, at that time.

The Continental Congress did not say how the stars should be arranged on the blue background, so flag makers used different designs. Sometimes, twelve stars were placed in a circle on the blue background with one star in the middle of the circle. Other times, the thirteen stars were placed in a circle on the blue background.

As new states became part of the United States, more stars and stripes were added to the flag. After awhile, people thought the flag had too many stripes. The Flag Act of 1818 stated the design of the American flag would include only thirteen stripes. The stripes were for the thirteen original colonies. The Flag Act also said the American flag should have one white star for each state that joins the United States. In 1846, the flag had 29 stars. By 1861, the number of stars had grown to 34, and in 1898, the flag contained 45 stars. The last change to the flag was in 1960 when a star was added for the state of Hawaii. On July 4 of that year, President Dwight D. Eisenhower approved the final arrangement of the 50 stars. The design of this 50-star flag is the one we still use today.

The American flag has had several nicknames over the years. Our country's earliest flag was known as the Continental flag or the Congress colors. Today, it is sometimes called the Stars and Stripes, Old Glory, or the Red, White, and Blue. No matter what name is used, the flag we see flying today is an important symbol of pride for our country.

Go On ▶

The American Flag

These are some examples of the American Flag. As you can see, there have been many different designs of the American Flag. Throughout the history of the United States, there have been more than 25 different designs. Here are just three examples.

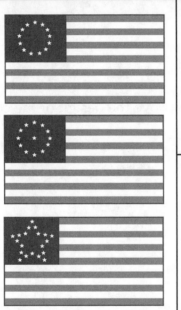

This is the current American Flag. The United States has used this design since 1960. The 50 stars represent our country's 50 states.

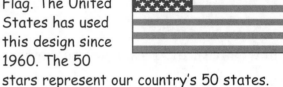

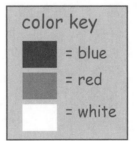

color key

= blue

= red

= white

Even though the American flag has had many designs, the colors have always been the same. Our flag includes red stripes, white stripes, white stars, and a blue square.

Now answer Numbers 1 through 6. Base your answers on the article "A Symbol of Pride" and the fact box "The American Flag."

1 Read this sentence from the passage.

> **The Continental Congress did not say how the stars should be arranged on the blue background, so flag makers used different designs.**

Which word has the SAME meaning as the word *arranged*?

Ⓐ makers

Ⓑ say

Ⓒ placed

Ⓓ moved

2 In what year did President Eisenhower approve the design of the current American flag?

Ⓕ 1777

Ⓖ 1861

Ⓗ 1960

Ⓘ 1898

3 How many stripes does the current American flag have?

Ⓐ fourteen

Ⓑ thirteen

Ⓒ seven

Ⓓ fifty

Go On

4 How are the flag of 1818 and the current American flag ALIKE?

   Ⓕ   The stars on both flags represent the original colonies.

   Ⓖ   The stripes on both flags represent cities in the United States.

   Ⓗ   The colors used on both flags are the same.

   Ⓘ   The colors used on both flags are red, white, and green.

5 Why did the author write "A Symbol of Pride"?

   Ⓐ   to tell readers about the history of the American flag

   Ⓑ   to tell readers about President Dwight Eisenhower

   Ⓒ   to tell readers about the Flag Act of 1818

   Ⓓ   to tell readers how to take care of a flag

6 Who said the original flag of the United States would have thirteen stripes?

   Ⓕ   President Eisenhower designed the flag with thirteen stripes.

   Ⓖ   The Flag Act of 1818 said the flag should have thirteen stripes.

   Ⓗ   The citizens of the United States voted to include thirteen stripes on the flag.

   Ⓘ   The Continental Congress said the flag would have thirteen stripes.

Read the story "Good Morning, Sunshine" before answering Numbers 7 through 12.

Good Morning, Sunshine

Annie woke up to a ray of sunlight on her face. She blinked her eyes and stretched her arms out from beneath her blankets. She couldn't believe it was morning already. It seemed as if she had just gone to sleep. Staring at the ceiling, she thought about her day and remembered what was going to happen in just two hours. Annie's stomach began to churn. She sat up but fell back onto her pillow. She closed her eyes again, secretly wishing it would all be over.

Her mother knocked and opened the bedroom door just a crack. She saw that Annie was awake. "Good morning, Sunshine. It's time to get up! You don't want to waste a second this morning."

But that's exactly what Annie wanted to do. Slowly, Annie pulled herself out of bed and looked around the room that was now hers. It was still a mess. Moving boxes were everywhere. Four white, empty walls stared back at her. Maybe it would be better when things were unpacked. That's what her mom and dad kept telling her. Annie couldn't believe it would ever feel as comfortable as her old room.

Go On ▶

Copying is Prohibited © Englefield & Associates, Inc.

The light of the sun made it possible to study each wall; it had been too dark the night before. One wall had a tiny crack that looked a little like a spider. "I'll never like a room with a spider crack," she thought to herself. Her mind was made up.

A pair of jeans, a purple shirt, and some sneakers—all brand new—were piled in the corner. Annie's mother surprised her daughter with the gift just yesterday. Annie knew her mother was trying to make her feel better, but Annie thought she might be more comfortable in her old clothes. New clothes never felt as good to her as her old ones. Since Annie didn't even know where to start looking for her old favorites, she settled for the new attire.

"Annie, I don't hear you moving. Are you up, Sunshine?"

"Why does she always call me that?" wondered Annie. It was a nickname Annie didn't like, but she had grown used to it. "She should call me 'Grumpy,' " Annie whispered to herself. "That's how I feel." With her shoes tied and her hair combed, she traveled into the unfamiliar hallway and down the stairs to greet a plate of pancakes.

"Oh, Annie, you look great!" her mom smiled as she poured a tall glass of milk.

"Thanks," Annie said, but she didn't really mean it. Around and around, she pushed syrup-soaked flapjacks around her plate. "How can I eat?" she thought. "My insides are tied in knots." Annie watched the clock count down the remaining moments of summer.

"Let's go, Annie." Her dad's voiced echoed. "You're going to miss the bus."

Now answer Numbers 7 through 12. Base your answers on the story "Good Morning, Sunshine."

7 Read this sentence from the story.

> **Since Annie didn't even know where to start looking for her old favorites, she settled for the new attire.**

Annie settled for

Ⓐ her favorite pair of jeans.

Ⓑ the new clothes.

Ⓒ an old shirt.

Ⓓ a new hat.

8 Why does Annie feel like her stomach is tied in knots?

Ⓕ She is nervous about her first day at a new school.

Ⓖ She doesn't like what she was going to have for breakfast.

Ⓗ She has to wear her old clothes to school instead of the new ones.

Ⓘ She doesn't feel well.

9 Why does Annie prefer the nickname "Grumpy"?

Ⓐ Her dad likes to call her "Grumpy."

Ⓑ Her mom likes to call her "Grumpy."

Ⓒ Annie feels grumpy.

Ⓓ Annie feels happy.

10 Why was Annie's room a mess?

Ⓕ She hasn't cleaned her room for two weeks.

Ⓖ She packed up all her things because she wants to paint the walls.

Ⓗ Her little brother made a mess the night before.

Ⓘ She and her family just moved into a new house.

11 How is Annie's new room DIFFERENT from her old room?

Ⓐ Annie's new room is more comfortable.

Ⓑ Annie's old room was a different color.

Ⓒ Annie's old room was bigger.

Ⓓ Annie's new room has a spider crack.

12 What woke up Annie?

Ⓕ her alarm clock

Ⓖ the sun

Ⓗ her mother

Ⓘ her father

Go On

Read the article "The Olympic Games" before answering Numbers 13 through 18.

The Olympic Games

Today, the Olympic Games include some of the most popular sporting events in the world. Many of the events we see in today's Olympics are based on games from ancient Greece—games played over two thousand years ago. Believe it or not, many of the sports we watch today also took place a long time ago.

The first Olympic Games were held thousands of years ago. People would travel for many miles to gather for the five-day festival. The Games began with an opening ceremony. Visitors would watch men compete in footraces, wrestling, horse and chariot races, and the pentathlon. The pentathlon was a combination of five events. Athletes ran, jumped, threw a discus, threw a javelin, and wrestled. Only men were allowed to take part in the ancient Olympics. The Olympics were held every fours years in the summer. Only summer sports were part of the ancient Games. Winners were given a crown made of leaves. The events of the original Olympic Games were stopped about 1,600 years ago, around the year 393.

The first modern Olympic Games were held in 1896. These Games took place in Athens, Greece. About 300 athletes competed (played) in the Games. Only summer events were included. The tradition of the Olympic Games has continued. The Summer Olympic Games include some of the same events as the ancient games. Athletes throw the discus and javelin, run in races of different lengths, and wrestle. The modern Olympics have many more sports. These include swimming, diving, tennis, volleyball, and many more.

The modern Olympic Games are different from the ancient Olympics in other ways, too. The Games now offer more than summer sports. The first Winter Olympics were held in 1924. Some Winter Olympic sports are skiing, skating, hockey, and basketball. The Summer and Winter Games still begin with an opening ceremony, but each is held in a different city every four years. Also, the Olympic athletes of today include both men and women. Another difference: winners receive medals in gold for first place, silver for second place, and bronze for third place finishes.

While many things have changed, the Olympic Games continue to be an event where people watch their favorite athletes compete to be the best in their events. It is a time when people come together to cheer, to compete, and to show pride in their abilities and in their countries.

Go On ▶

Copying is Prohibited   © Englefield & Associates, Inc.

Now answer Numbers 13 through 18. Base your answers on the article "The Olympic Games."

13 Read this sentence from the article.

> **Many of the events we see in today's Olympics are based on games from ancient Greece.**

What does the word *ancient* mean?

Ⓐ   long ago

Ⓑ   well organized

Ⓒ   popular

Ⓓ   dusty and dirty

14 How are the ancient Olympics and the modern Olympics ALIKE?

Ⓕ   Both included men and women.

Ⓖ   Both had races, volleyball, and tennis.

Ⓗ   Both included summer and winter sports.

Ⓘ   Both awarded prizes to winners.

15 Why did the author write "The Olympic Games"?

Ⓐ   to inform the reader about the first Olympic Games in Greece

Ⓑ   to give information about the summer Olympic Games

Ⓒ   to explain when the Olympic Games became popular

Ⓓ   to explain how the modern Olympics and the ancient Olympics are alike and different

16 The winners of the FIRST Olympic Games were given

    Ⓕ   a gold medal.

    Ⓖ   a crown of leaves.

    Ⓗ   a necklace of leaves.

    Ⓘ   a gold crown.

17 What is a pentathlon?

    Ⓐ   a uniform worn by athletes

    Ⓑ   another name for the opening ceremonies

    Ⓒ   five running and throwing events in the summer Olympics

    Ⓓ   a game played by women in ancient Greece

18 The modern Olympics are DIFFERENT from the ancient Olympics because

    Ⓕ   the ancient Olympics included winter sports.

    Ⓖ   the modern Olympics include winter sports.

    Ⓗ   the modern Olympics do not honor winners.

    Ⓘ   the ancient Olympics included women.

Go On

Read the story "Tony's Skunk" before answering Numbers 19 through 24.

Tony's Skunk

Tony had never been so scared. The light of his flashlight was fixed on a small animal. The bright eyes of a skunk stared at him. "You're smaller than my puppy," he whispered. He knew the animal wouldn't attack him. Yet, he was afraid to move a muscle. "What am I going to do?" he thought. Tony knew if he did the wrong thing, he would be very sorry.

This was the first time Tony had spotted a skunk. Tony didn't know much about the black and white creature, but he knew he must be careful. When skunks are scared, they spray a liquid that smells very bad. This liquid, which comes from a gland near the base of the tail, keeps predators away. Tony knew the skunk would growl and stomp its feet if it was about to spray. So, he carefully watched the little animal.

The skunk seemed startled. "He's as scared as I am," Tony thought. Tony's eyes were locked on the skunk. The skunk's eyes were fixed on Tony. A few more moments passed. Tony was ready to make a decision. "I hope I'm doing the right thing."

Tony began to move away slowly. He never let his eyes leave the skunk. He picked up his right foot, then his left. He softly whispered to himself, "I don't want to hurt you. Just let me get away from you."

The skunk was motionless. Tony moved away from him. Inch by inch, Tony backed away through the brush. He didn't want to move his flashlight off the skunk. He couldn't see where he was walking. He hoped he didn't stumble and fall. The leaves softly crunched under his feet. The skunk remained motionless.

He started to feel a bit of relief. Tony was about twelve feet from the little animal. He continued to step gently. Then suddenly, his foot came down and "CRACK!" The sound echoed about. It was only a dry stick, but it made Tony jump. The flashlight hit the ground. Light bounced around the brush. Tony's heart was beating fast. He couldn't see the skunk. The light no longer hit the skunk's eyes. Tony heard a small growl. "Oh no! I'm going to get it!" But Tony was lucky; the skunk had different plans. Tony heard four small footsteps running through the brush. Relieved, Tony scooped up his flashlight and quickly headed in the opposite direction.

Go On ▶

Now answer Numbers 19 through 24. Base your answers on the story "Tony's Skunk."

19 Why was Tony scared?

    (A)   He thought the skunk might bite him.

    (B)   The light on his flashlight did not work.

    (C)   He thought the skunk might spray him.

    (D)   He was lost in the woods.

20 What happened AFTER Tony stepped on the dry stick?

    (F)   Tony saw the skunk.

    (G)   Tony dropped his flashlight.

    (H)   The skunk sprayed Tony.

    (I)   Tony's foot hurt.

21 How are Tony and the skunk ALIKE?

    (A)   They both were afraid.

    (B)   They both like the woods.

    (C)   They both have black hair.

    (D)   They both growled at each other.

22 How does Tony try to solve his problem with the skunk?

    Ⓕ   He throws his flashlight at the skunk.

    Ⓖ   He growls at the skunk to scare it.

    Ⓗ   He slowly steps away from the skunk.

    Ⓘ   He cracks a stick to scare the skunk.

23 When Tony first steps away from the skunk, he is unable to see where he is walking because

    Ⓐ   he dropped his flashlight.

    Ⓑ   his flashlight does not have batteries.

    Ⓒ   Tony forgot his flashlight at home.

    Ⓓ   the flashlight is pointed at the skunk.

24 How does Tony let the reader know the size of the skunk?

    Ⓕ   Tony says the skunk is smaller than his puppy.

    Ⓖ   Tony says the skunk is only nine inches tall.

    Ⓗ   Tony says the skunk is shorter than his flashlight.

    Ⓘ   Tony says the skunk is the smallest skunk he has ever seen.

Read the story "Carrots and Gravy" before answering Numbers 25 through 32.

There are two foods I never want to see on my plate: carrots and gravy. I don't mean together. I dislike them separately. For as long as I can remember, I have never liked these two. I'm not sure why. Mom says, even when I was little, carrots and gravy weren't for me.

We have a special rule in our house. At dinner, we have to try everything on our plates. I've tried carrots with salad and gravy with potatoes, but nothing works. I'm nine years old, and I still don't like carrots or gravy. I know I never will. A few weeks ago, carrots were served, again. I complained, but mom just looked at me. I knew the rule. I swallowed the orange mess. I grabbed my throat. I grabbed by belly. I fell from my chair. Mom just looked at me.

"I guess he's tried long enough. If Julio survives, no more carrots. I promise."

I lifted my head off the floor. "What about gravy?" I smiled.

"We'll see."

Mom kept her promise, and all was going great until a special family dinner. Mom and I met my grandparents at their favorite restaurant. We were celebrating their wedding anniversary. My uncle and his son Jake were there, too. Jake is a year older; he's in fourth grade. Jake and I both wanted hamburgers and french fries with lots of ketchup. We sat at the table, practicing our orders. A waitress came by and served a few glasses of water.

"Your dinners will be ready, soon."

"But we haven't ordered, yet." Jake and I were confused.

"It's been taken care of," she said. "I just know you're going to love it."

My uncle had called ahead to save time. I was disappointed. I was really looking forward to my hamburger.

Copying is Prohibited   © Englefield & Associates, Inc.

The waitress was right. Our dinner started in no time at all. The salad came first, but it was piled with little carrot slices. I tried to be polite. I pushed the orange pieces to the side of my plate. When my salad was free of carrots, I enjoyed every last bite. "This isn't so bad," I thought.

After taking away our salad plates, it was time for the main course. "Please!" I whispered to Jake, "let it be something I like!" I held my breath. The plate was in front of me. I peeked. Turkey and mashed potatoes covered in gravy! Mom smiled at me. I didn't grab my throat or my belly. Instead, I shrugged my shoulder and gave her half a smile. I spent most of the dinner just moving things around on my plate. Everyone was busy talking. No one seemed to notice.

"Are you going to eat that?" Jake asked. I shook my head no. He heaped the dinner onto his plate. "This stuff is great." I couldn't believe he thought so. All that gravy—yuck.

I thought my mom would be mad, but on our way home, she stopped at Happy Burger. I didn't even ask her to. "What will you have, Julio?" Mom asked.

"I'll take a cheeseburger and fries. No carrots. No gravy."

Now answer Numbers 25 through 32. Base your answers on the story "Carrots and Gravy."

25 Why did Julio's mom stop at Happy Burger?

Ⓐ   She had a coupon for free french fries.

Ⓑ   She knew Julio didn't eat much at the restaurant.

Ⓒ   She was hungry.

Ⓓ   She took Julio to Happy Burger to celebrate his birthday.

26 When Julio was served something he didn't like at the restaurant, he

Ⓕ   complained to everyone at the table.

Ⓖ   grabbed his throat and his belly and fell to the floor.

Ⓗ   ordered something else from the menu.

Ⓘ   pushed his food around his plate.

27 How are Julio and Jake ALIKE?

Ⓐ   They both wanted to order hamburgers.

Ⓑ   They both enjoyed the dinner at the restaurant.

Ⓒ   They are the same age.

Ⓓ   They both go to the same school.

28 Read this sentence from the story.

He heaped the dinner onto his plate.

When Jake *heaped* Julio's dinner onto his plate, he

Ⓕ threw Julio's dinner at him.

Ⓖ piled Julio's dinner on his plate.

Ⓗ ate Julio's dinner.

Ⓘ stole Julio's dinner plate.

29 What is the FIRST thing served at the restaurant?

Ⓐ turkey and mashed potatoes with gravy

Ⓑ salads with carrots on top

Ⓒ glasses of water

Ⓓ hamburgers and french fries

30 Why did the author write "Carrots and Gravy"?

Ⓕ to tell readers to try all foods on their plates

Ⓖ to tell a story about Julio, a boy who doesn't like carrots or gravy

Ⓗ to tell readers they should eat at Happy Burger instead of at nice restaurants

Ⓘ to tell a story about why Julio has to eat carrots and gravy

31 At the restaurant, Julio's mom smiles at him, and he gives her half a smile. They do this because they BOTH

  (A)   know Julio doesn't like the main course.

  (B)   don't like the main course.

  (C)   know Jake doesn't like the main course.

  (D)   are happy to share the special day with Julio's grandparents.

32 How do you know Julio's mom is not mad at him when he doesn't eat his dinner at the restaurant?

  (F)   She fixes him a hamburger when they get home from the restaurant.

  (G)   She lets him eat dessert, even though he didn't finish the main course.

  (H)   She tells him she is not mad at him.

  (I)   She stops at Happy Burger to get him some food.

Read the article "Journal Writing" before answering Numbers 33 through 40.

Writing in a journal is a great way to keep track of things in your life. A journal can also be called a diary. Writers use journals to record their thoughts and ideas. Some people use journals to collect story ideas. Others write about bad days or happy times. Keeping a journal can help you reflect or think about what is happening in your life. When you read what you have written in your journal, you can learn from your everyday experiences.

It doesn't take any fancy materials to start a journal. You can start with a simple notebook and a pen or a pencil. You can get a special notebook if you want to make your journal more fancy. You can also use a computer to start your journal. The important thing is to record your thoughts and ideas. You can write them on paper or you can type them, whichever way is the best for you.

Try to write in your journal every day. You don't need to write for a long period of time, maybe only five or ten minutes, at first. As you keep practicing, you may find that you want to write for a few more minutes.

Journal Ideas

Write about things that happen each day.

Write about books you have read.

Keep a dialogue journal.
You and another person (a friend, parent, or teacher) write back and forth to each other.

Write stories.

Write about something new you learn each day.

Journal Materials

computer

notebook and pencil

Important Things to Remember

Write every day.

June 9, 2007
Write the date on each piece.

Review what you have written.

Practice good writing skills.

Writing a journal is a good way to practice your writing skills. Even though your journal is filled with your own words, try to use your best handwriting (if you're writing in a notebook). You want to be able to read what you have written! Also, try to spell words correctly and use complete sentences. Working on these skills will help you become a better writer.

Another secret to journal writing is to keep track of your writing. Put the date on each piece. This will help you remember when things happened. Every week or so, go back and read what you have written. You might find that something that seemed important has been forgotten. You might also find words that surprise you. Whatever the case, keep writing. You may be surprised at how much you have to say.

Go On ▶

Now answer Numbers 33 through 40. Base your answers on the article "Journal Writing."

33 What materials do you need to begin journal writing?

   Ⓐ   You need several fancy notebooks and pens.

   Ⓑ   You need two notebooks and fancy pencils.

   Ⓒ   You need paper and something to write with.

   Ⓓ   You need a computer because journals must be typed.

34 What is the purpose of the article?

   Ⓕ   to explain how to begin keeping a journal

   Ⓖ   to persuade you that a diary is the best type of journal

   Ⓗ   to describe what a dialogue journal is

   Ⓘ   to tell about a personal experience in a journal

35 Which of the following is NOT something to remember when journal writing?

   Ⓐ   Write the date on each piece.

   Ⓑ   Review what you have written.

   Ⓒ   Practice good writing skills.

   Ⓓ   Always write with a blue pen.

36 How often does this author think you should write in your journal?

  Ⓕ   once a week

  Ⓖ   twice a day

  Ⓗ   once a day

  Ⓘ   once an hour

37 The author says a journal is LIKE a

  Ⓐ   computer.

  Ⓑ   pencil.

  Ⓒ   diary.

  Ⓓ   teacher.

38 Read this sentence from the article.

  This will help you remember when things happened.

  Which word is the OPPOSITE of the word *remember*?

  Ⓕ   think about

  Ⓖ   review

  Ⓗ   forget

  Ⓘ   recall

39 Why does the author say you should use your best handwriting if you're writing in a notebook?

    Ⓐ   You want others to be able to read what you have written.

    Ⓑ   You want to be able to read what you have written.

    Ⓒ   The author does not like messy handwriting.

    Ⓓ   You want your writing to look pretty on the page.

40 Which journal topic is NOT mentioned?

    Ⓕ   a book you recently read

    Ⓖ   something new you learned today

    Ⓗ   a special story

    Ⓘ   a description of your house

Read the story "The Key" before answering Numbers 41 through 46.

The Key

Emma noticed a small, white box on the stairs. She picked it up carefully and opened it to find a small key wrapped in a lace handkerchief. Faded pink and blue flowers decorated the delicate handkerchief, and the initials "A.B." were stitched into one corner. Emma assumed that it could belong to her grandmother because her name, Abby Brown, matched the initials.

As Emma examined the key, she saw that it was a dull, golden color. It was about as long as her index finger and seemed heavy for its size. There was a bit of crumpled blue ribbon looped through the hole at the top of the key. Emma thought to herself that the key must be very old because it was so worn. Emma wanted to find her grandmother and ask her about the key. As she went from room to room looking for her grandmother, Emma imagined that there might be wonderful treasures somewhere for that key to unlock. Then, Emma remembered that Gramma had gone to the store. Emma's questions would have to wait until she returned.

Emma was sitting on the porch step when Gramma returned. She slowly removed the key from her pocket and held it up for Gramma to see. "Look what I found—is it yours?" Emma asked. A broad smile appeared on Gramma's face as she inspected the key. "I thought I had lost this," Gramma said. "This key opens a very special box I have stored in the attic." Then, Gramma took Emma's hand and said, "Come with me. I have something to show you."

Emma and her grandmother walked through the house to the back stairs that led up to the attic. As they climbed the steep steps to the storage place, Emma's mind raced with thoughts about that special box. She pondered what it would look like and, most importantly, what would be inside the box.

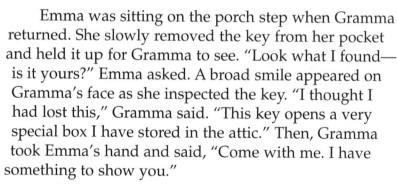

Go On ▶

Copying is Prohibited   © Englefield & Associates, Inc.

Now answer Numbers 41 through 46. Base your answers on the story "The Key."

41 Where was Emma waiting when her grandmother returned?

Ⓐ inside the house

Ⓑ in the backyard

Ⓒ on the porch

Ⓓ in the car

42 Read this sentence from the story.

She pondered what it would look like and, most importantly, what would be inside the box.

Which word means almost the SAME as *pondered*?

Ⓕ worried

Ⓖ wondered

Ⓗ guessed

Ⓘ denied

43 What event happens AFTER Emma sits on the porch?

Ⓐ Emma finds the old key.

Ⓑ Emma finds a crumpled blue ribbon.

Ⓒ Emma imagines that she would find treasure.

Ⓓ Emma shows her grandmother the key that she found.

Go On ▶

44 Read this sentence from the story.

> **Emma assumed that it could belong to her grandmother because her name, Abby Brown, matched the initials.**

What does the word *assumed* mean?

(F) didn't believe

(G) remembered

(H) guessed

(I) wondered

45 What is the MAIN idea of the second paragraph?

(A) Emma examines the key.

(B) Emma finds the key.

(C) Emma searches for her grandmother.

(D) Emma waits for her grandmother.

46 How are Emma and Gramma ALIKE?

(F) Both Emma and Gramma are nervous about what is inside of the special box.

(G) Both Emma and Gramma are excited about what is inside of the special box.

(H) Both Emma and Gramma are scared about what is inside of the special box.

(I) Both Emma and Gramma do not care about what is inside of the special box.

Go On ▶

Read the article "The Hidden Message" before answering Numbers 47 through 50.

THE HIDDEN MESSAGE

Secret messages aren't just for detectives and spies. Some of them, the kinds that use words in place of other words or put letters in a different order, can be very hard. These are the types of secret messages that kings and rulers used when messages had to be carried on foot or by horse. If an enemy caught a soldier carrying one of these secret correspondences, the person sending the message hoped that the enemy would not be able to read it.

Because the messages sent out by kings and rulers were usually very important, the people who were writing the secret codes wanted to make them hard to read. Not all secret codes have to be so hard, though. There are some ways that you can make simple secret messages to send to your friends.

One way you can send secret messages is to use invisible ink. Invisible ink can be made in a few different ways. One way is to use lemon juice to write on a piece of paper. You can write by dipping a toothpick or the tip of a dried-out pen into the lemon juice, then use it to write as you would normally. Let the juice dry completely and give the secret message to a friend. The friend will need a parent or another adult to help read the message. Have the parent or adult hold the message up close to a light bulb, or have them hold a hot iron an inch or two above the paper. When the paper gets hot, the lemon juice will darken and the message will appear.

There is another way to write an invisible message using only art supplies. Write on a piece of white paper with a white crayon. It may be difficult to see what you are writing, but when you're done, it will look like nothing is there. Anyone who wants to read the message can use water-based paint to paint over the side with the writing on it. The secret message will appear.

Go On ▶

Now answer Numbers 47 through 50. Base your answers on the article "The Hidden Message."

47 When the paper becomes hot, what happens to the lemon juice?

Ⓐ   It starts to smell.

Ⓑ   It begins to melt.

Ⓒ   It disappears.

Ⓓ   It turns darker.

48 One reason kings wrote in secret code was

Ⓕ   to protect important information.

Ⓖ   to trick the messenger.

Ⓗ   to entertain themselves.

Ⓘ   because they couldn't read.

49 Why did the author write "The Hidden Message"?

Ⓐ   to tell how to send invisible messages to friends

Ⓑ   to get the reader to tell more secrets

Ⓒ   to tell readers how kings and rulers sent messages

Ⓓ   to explain the different uses of lemon juice

50 Read this sentence from the article.

Invisible ink can be made in a few different ways.

Which word means the OPPOSITE of *invisible*?

(F)   visible

(G)   hidden

(H)   secret

(I)   covered

This is the end of the Reading Assessment.
Until time is called, go back and check your work or answer questions you did
not complete. When you have finished, close your workbook.

BLANK PAGE

Mathematics

Introduction

In the Mathematics section of the Florida Comprehensive Assessment Test (FCAT), you will be asked questions designed to test what you have learned in school. These questions have been written based on the mathematics you have been taught in school through third grade. The questions you answer are not meant to confuse or to trick you but are written so you have the best opportunity to show what you know about mathematics.

The *Show What You Know® on the 3rd Grade FCAT, Student Workbook* includes a Mathematics Practice Tutorial that will help you practice your test-taking skills. Following the Mathematics Practice Tutorial is a full-length Mathematics Assessment.

About the FCAT Mathematics for Grade 3

Items in this section of the FCAT will test your ability to perform mathematical tasks in real-world and mathematical situations, and will neither require you to define mathematical terminology nor memorize specific facts. The FCAT is meant to gauge your ability to apply mathematical concepts to a given situation. This will include the addition, subtraction, multiplication, and division of whole numbers; addition and subtraction of decimals; addition and subtraction of simple fractions; and measurement.

The Assessment will contain 45–50 Mathematics questions and you will be given 120 minutes to complete the Assessment.

Item Distribution and Scoring

The 3rd Grade FCAT Mathematics uses only multiple-choice items.

You will select from four possible answer choices and fill in a bubble in your answer book. Although multiple-choice items sometimes ask for the recall of facts, most of the sample items demand a more complex thought process. Each multiple-choice item on the Assessment is scored 0 (incorrect) or 1 (correct). Each correct answer adds one point to the total assessment score.

The following chart shows the approximate percent of raw-score points taken from each Mathematic Content Category.

Mathematics Content Categories	Points
Number Sense, Concepts, and Operations	30%
Measurement	20%
Geometry and Spacial Sense	17%
Algebraic Thinking	15%
Data Analysis	18%

Glossary

acute angle: An angle that measures less than 90 degrees and greater than 0 degrees.

addend: Numbers added together to give a sum. For example, 2 + 7 = 9. The numbers 2 and 7 are addends.

addition: An operation joining two or more sets where the result is the whole.

algebraic equation (inequality): A mathematical sentence that may contain variables, constants, and operation symbols in which two expressions are connected by an equality (or inequality) symbol.

algebraic expression: An expression containing numbers and variables (e.g., $7x$), and operations that involve numbers and variables (e.g., $2x + y$). Algebraic expressions may or may not contain equality or inequality symbols.

algebraic order of operations: The order in which computations are made in an algebraic expression. The order is: parentheses, multiplication/division (from left to right), addition/subtraction (from left to right).

algebraic rule: A mathematical expression containing variables and describing a pattern or relationship.

A.M.: The hours from midnight to noon; from Latin words *ante meridiem* meaning before noon.

analyze: To break down information into parts so that it may be more easily understood.

angle: A figure formed by two rays that meet at the same end point called a vertex. Angles can be obtuse, acute, right, or straight, and are measured in degrees.

area: The number of square units needed to cover the inside region of a closed two-dimensional figure. The most common abbreviation for area is A.

Associative Property of Addition: The grouping of addends can be changed and the sum will be the same. Example: (3 + 1) + 2 = 6; 3 + (1 + 2) = 6.

Associative Property of Multiplication: The grouping of factors can be changed and the product will be the same. Example: (3 x 2) x 4 = 24; 3 x (2 x 4) = 24.

attribute: A characteristic or distinctive feature.

average: A number found by adding two or more quantities together and then dividing the sum by the number of quantities. For example, in the set {9, 5, 4}, the average is 6: 9 + 5 + 4 = 18; 18 ÷ 3 = 6. *See mean.*

axes: Plural of axis. Perpendicular lines used as reference lines in a coordinate plane system or graph; traditionally, the horizontal axis (x-axis) represents the independent variable and the vertical axis (y-axis) represents the dependent variable.

bar graph: A graph using either vertical or horizontal bars to show data.

base (geometric): Usually refers to the side of a polygon closest to the bottom of the page. It is from the base that height can be measured.

break: A zigzag or v-shape on the x- or y-axis in a line or bar graph that indicates the data being displayed does not include all of the values that exist in the number line used. Breaks are very useful when there is a large difference between high and low values in the data set, or when specific values need to be excluded from the scale. Also called a squiggle.

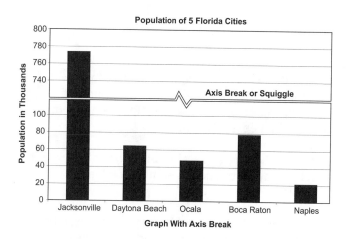

Graph With Axis Break

capacity: The amount an object holds when filled.

chart: A way to show information, such as in a graph or table.

Glossary

circle: Closed, curved line made up of points that are all the same distance from a point inside called the center. Example: A circle with center point P is shown below.

circle graph: Sometimes called a pie chart; a way of representing data that shows the fractional part or percentage of an overall set as an appropriately-sized wedge of a circle. Example:

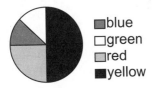

blue
green
red
yellow

circumference: The boundary line or perimeter of a circle; also, the length of the perimeter of a circle. Example:

Circumference

closed figure: A two-dimensional figure that divides the plane where the figure lies into two parts—the part inside the figure and the part outside the figure (e.g., circles, squares, triangles).

Commutative Property of Addition: Numbers can be added in any order and the sum will be the same. Example: 3 + 4 = 4 + 3.

Commutative Property of Multiplication: Numbers can be multiplied in any order and the product will be the same. Example: 3 x 6 = 6 x 3.

compare: To look for similarities and differences. For example, is one number greater than, less than, or equal to another number?

composite number: A number that has more than two factors. Examples include 4, 35, and 121. The numbers 0 and 1 are not composite numbers.

conclusion: A statement that follows logically from other facts.

cone: A solid figure with a circle as its base and a curved surface that meets at a point.

cones

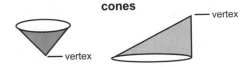

vertex

vertex

congruent figures: Figures that have the same shape and size.

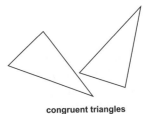

congruent triangles

coordinate grid or plane: A two-dimensional arrangement of parallel and evenly-spaced horizontal and vertical lines that is designed for locating points or displaying data.

coordinates: Ordered pairs of numbers that identify the location of points on a coordinate plane. Example: (3, 4) is the coordinate of point A.

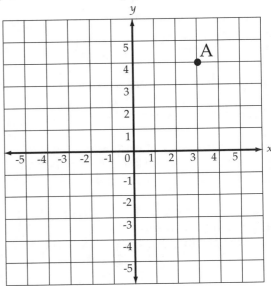

Copying is Prohibited

© Englefield & Associates, Inc.

Glossary

cube: A solid figure with six faces that are congruent (equal) squares.

cylinder: A solid figure with two circular bases that are congruent (equal) and parallel to each other connected by a curved lateral surface.

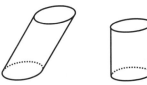

data: Information that is collected.

decimal number: A number written with a decimal point that is expressed in base 10, such as 39,456 where each digit's value is determined by multiplying it by some power of ten.

denominator: The bottom number in a fraction.

diagram: A drawing that represents a mathematical situation.

diameter: A line segment (or length of a segment) passing through the center of the circle with end points on the circle.

difference: The answer when subtracting two numbers.

direct measure: Obtaining the measure of an object by using a measuring device, such as a ruler, yardstick, meter stick, tape measure, scale, thermometer, measuring cup, or some other tool. Nonstandard devices, such as a paper clip or pencil may also be used.

distance: The length between two points.

dividend: A number in a division problem that is divided. Dividend ÷ divisor = quotient. Example: In 15 ÷ 3 = 5, 15 is the dividend.

$$\overset{\text{quotient}}{\text{divisor}\overline{)\text{dividend}}} \qquad 3\overline{)\,15\,}^{\,5}$$

divisible: A number that can be divided by another number without leaving a remainder. Example: 12 is divisible by 3 because 12 ÷ 3 is an integer, namely 4.

division: An operation that tells how many equal groups there are or how many are in each group.

divisor: The number by which another number is divided. Example: In 15 ÷ 3 = 5, 3 is the divisor.

$$\overset{\text{quotient}}{\text{divisor}\overline{)\text{dividend}}} \qquad 3\overline{)\,15\,}^{\,5}$$

edge: The line segment where two faces of a solid figure meet.

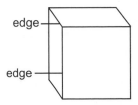

equality: Two or more sets of values that are equal.

equation: A number sentence that says two expressions are equal (=). Example: 4 + 8 = 6 + 6.

equivalent forms of a number: The same number expressed in different forms (e.g., $\frac{3}{4}$, 0.75, 75%).

equivalent fractions: Two fractions with equal values.

estimate: To find an approximate value or measurement of something without exact calculation.

evaluate an algebraic expression: Substitute numbers for the variables in the expression, then follow the algebraic order of operations to find the numerical value of the expression.

even number: A whole number that has a 0, 2, 4, 6, or 8 in the ones place. A number that is a multiple of 2. Examples: 0, 4, and 678 are even numbers.

expanded form: A number written as the sum of the values of its digits. Example: 546 = 500 + 40 + 6.

expression: A combination of variables, numbers, and symbols that represents a mathematical relationship.

extraneous information: Information not needed to solve the problem.

Glossary

face: One side of a three-dimensional figure. For example, a cube has six faces that are all squares. The pyramid below has five faces—four triangles and one square.

face

factor: One of two or more numbers that are multiplied together to give a product. Example: In 4 x 3 = 12, 4 and 3 are factors of 12.

fact family: A group of related facts using the same numbers. Example: 5 + 8 = 13; 13 − 8 = 5.

figure: A geometric figure is a set of points and/or lines in 2 or 3 dimensions.

flip (reflection): The change in a position of a figure that is the result of picking it up and turning it over. Example: Reversing a "b" to a "d." Tipping a "p" to a "b" or a "b" to a "p" as shown below:

fraction: A symbol, such as $\frac{2}{8}$ or $\frac{5}{3}$, used to name a part of a whole, a part of a set, or a location on the number line. Examples:

$$\frac{numerator}{denominator} = \frac{dividend}{divisor} =$$

$$\frac{\text{\# of parts under consideration}}{\text{\# of parts in a set}}$$

function: A relationship, such as a graph, in which a variable, called the dependent variable, is dependent on another value, usually an independent variable. In a function, each value of *x* corresponds to only one value of *y*.

function machine: Applies a function rule to a set of numbers, which determines a corresponding set of numbers. Example: Input 9 → Rule x 7 → Output 63. If you apply the function rule "multiply by 7" to the values 5, 7, and 9, the corresponding values are:

5 → 35
7 → 49
9 → 63

graph: A picture showing how certain facts are related to each other or how they compare to one another. Some examples of types of graphs are line graphs, pie charts, bar graphs, scatterplots, and pictographs.

grid: A pattern of regularly spaced horizontal and vertical lines on a plane that can be used to locate points and graph equations.

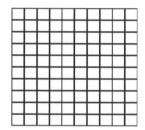

height: A line segment drawn from any vertex of a polygon to any side so that the line is perpendicular to the side to which it is drawn.

hexagon: A six-sided polygon. The total measure of the angles within a hexagon is 720°.

regular hexagon   irregular hexagons

impossible event: An event that can never happen.

indirect measure: To obtain data about an object by measuring another object or doing some calculation that allows you to infer what the actual measurement must be.

inequality: Two or more sets of values are not equal. There are a number of specific inequality types, including less than (<), greater than (>), and not equal to (≠).

Glossary

integer: Any number, positive or negative, that is a whole number distance away from zero on a number line, in addition to zero. Specifically, an integer is any number in the set {. . .-3,-2,-1, 0, 1, 2, 3. . .}. Examples of integers include 1, 5, 273, -2, -35, and -1,375.

intersecting lines: Lines that cross at a point. Examples:

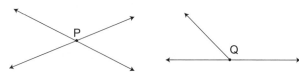

inverse operation: An action that undergoes a previously applied action. For example, subtraction is the inverse operation of addition.

isosceles triangle: A triangle with at least two sides that are the same length.

justify: To prove or show to be true or valid using logic and/or evidence.

key: An explanation of what each symbol represents in a pictograph.

kilometer (km): A metric unit of length. 1 kilometer = 1,000 meters.

labels (for a graph): The titles given to a graph, the axes of a graph, or to the scales on the axes of a graph.

length: A one-dimensional measure that is the measurable property of line segments.

likelihood: The chance that something is likely to happen.

line: A straight path of points that goes on forever in both directions.

line graph: A graph that uses a line or a curve to show how data changes over time.

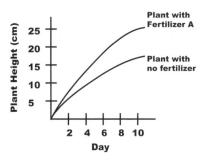

line of symmetry: A line on which a figure can be folded into two parts so that the parts match exactly.

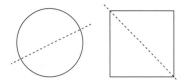

line segment: A part of a line with a beginning and an end point.

liter (L): A metric unit of capacity. 1 liter = 1,000 milliliters.

mass: The amount of matter in an object.

mean: Also called arithmetic average. A number found by adding two or more quantities together, and then dividing the sum by the number of quantities. For example, in the set {9, 5, 4} the mean is 6: 9 + 5 + 4 = 18; 18 ÷ 3 = 6. *See average.*

median: The middle number when numbers are put in order from least to greatest or from greatest to least. For example, in the set of numbers 6, 7, 8, 9, 10, the number 8 is the median (middle) number.

meter (m): A metric unit of length. 1 meter = 100 centimeters.

method: A systematic way of accomplishing a task.

mixed number: A number consisting of a whole number and a fraction. Example: $6\frac{2}{3}$.

Glossary

mode: The number or numbers that occur most often in a set of data. Example: The mode of {1, 3, 4, 5, 5, 7, 9} is 5.

multiple: A product of a number and any other whole number. Examples: {2, 4, 6, 8, 10, 12,...} are multiples of 2.

multiplication: An operation on two numbers that tells how many in all. The first number is the number of sets and the second number tells how many in each set.

natural numbers (counting numbers): The set of positive integers used for counting {1, 2, 3, 4, 5,...}.

nonstandard units of measure: Objects, such as blocks, paper clips or pencils, that can be used to measure objects.

number line: A line that shows numbers in order using a scale. Equal intervals are marked and usually labeled on the number line.

number sentence: An expression of a relationship between quantities as an equation or an inequality. Examples: 7 + 7 = 8 + 6; 14 < 92; 56 + 4 > 59.

numerator: The top number in a fraction.

obtuse angle: An angle with a measure greater than 90 degrees and less than 180 degrees.

octagon: An eight-sided polygon. The total measure of the angles within an octagon is 1,080°.

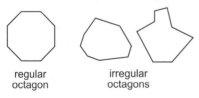

regular
octagon

irregular
octagons

odd number: A whole number that has 1, 3, 5, 7, or 9 in the ones place. An odd number is not divisible by 2. Examples: The numbers 53 and 701 are odd numbers.

operation: A mathematical process that combines numbers; basic operations of arithmetic include addition, subtraction, multiplication, and division.

order: To arrange numbers from the least to greatest or from the greatest to least.

ordered pair: Two numbers inside a set of parentheses separated by a comma that are used to name a point on a coordinate grid. Example: (2, 5).

organized data: Data arranged in a way that is meaningful and that assists in the interpretation of that data.

parallelogram: A quadrilateral in which opposite sides are parallel.

parallel lines: Lines in the same plane that never intersect.

pattern: An arrangement of numbers, pictures, etc., in an organized and predictable way. Examples: 3, 6, 9, 12 or ® 0 ® 0 ® 0.

pentagon: A five-sided polygon. The total measure of the angles within a pentagon is 540°.

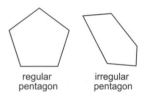

regular
pentagon

irregular
pentagon

percent: A ratio of a number to 100. Percent means per hundred and is represented by the symbol %. Example: "35 to 100" means 35%.

perimeter: The distance around a figure.

perpendicular lines: Two lines that intersect to form a right angle (90 degrees).

90°

Glossary

pictograph: A graph that uses pictures or symbols to represent similar data. The value of each picture is interpreted by a "key" or "legend."

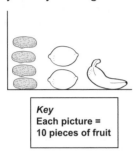

Key
Each picture =
10 pieces of fruit

place value: The value given to the place a digit has in a number. Example: In the number 135, the 1 is in the hundreds place so it represents 100 (1 x 100), the 3 is in the tens place so it represents 30 (3 x 10), and the 5 is in the ones place so it represents 5 (5 x 1).

plane: Any region that can be defined by a minimum of three noncollinear points and that extends infinitely in a two-dimensional manner. It's like an infinite piece of paper with no thickness.

plane figure: An arrangement of points, lines, or curves within a single plane, a "flat" figure.

P.M.: The hours from noon to midnight; from the Latin words *post meridiem* meaning after noon.

point: An exact position often marked by a dot.

polygon: A closed figure made up of straight line segments.

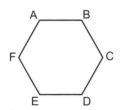

ABCDEF is a polygon.

possible event: An event that might or might not happen.

predict: To tell what you believe may happen in the future.

prediction: A description of what may happen before it happens.

prime number: A whole number greater than 1 having exactly two whole number factors, itself, and 1. Examples: The number 7 is prime since its only whole number factors are 1 and 7. One is not a prime number.

probability: The likelihood that something will happen.

product: The answer to a multiplication problem. Example: In 3 x 4 = 12, 12 is the product.

pyramid: A solid figure in which the base is a polygon and whose faces are triangles with a common point called a vertex.

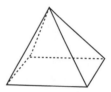

quadrilateral: A four-sided polygon. Rectangles, squares, parallelograms, rhombi, and trapezoids are all quadrilaterals. The total measure of the angles within a quadrilateral is 360º. Example: ABCD is a quadrilateral.

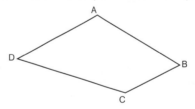

questionnaire: A set of questions for a survey.

quotient: The answer in a division problem. Dividend ÷ divisor = quotient. Example: In 15 ÷ 3 = 5, 5 is the quotient.

radius: The distance from the center to the edge of a circle; or, the distance from the center of a circle to a point on the circle.

randomly (chosen): When all items within a set have an equal chance of being chosen.

Glossary

range: The difference between the least number and the greatest number in a data set. For example, in the set {4, 7, 10, 12, 36, 7, 2}, the range is 34. The greatest number (36) minus the least number (2): (36 − 2 = 34).

ratio: A comparison of two numbers using a variety of written forms. Example: The ratio of two and five may be written "2 to 5" or 2:5 or 2/5.

ray: A straight line extending infinitely in one direction from a given point.

rectangle: A quadrilateral with four right angles. A square is one example of a rectangle.

reflection: The change in the position of a figure that is the result of picking it up and turning it over. *See flip.*

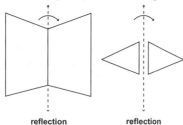

reflection   reflection

regular polygon: A special type of polygon that is both equilateral and equiangular.

relative size: The size of one number in comparison to another number or numbers.

represent: To present clearly; describe; show.

remainder: The number that is left over after dividing. Example: In 31 ÷ 7 = 4 R 3, the 3 is the remainder.

rhombus: A quadrilateral with opposite sides parallel and all sides the same length. A square is one kind of rhombus.

right angle: An angle that forms a square corner and measures 90 degrees.

right prism or rectangular solid: A three-dimensional figure (polyhedron) with congruent, polygonal or rectangular bases, and lateral faces that are all rectangles.

right triangle: A triangle having one right angle. *See angle* and *triangle.*

rotation: Moving an object around an imaginary point in a circular motion either clockwise or counterclockwise. After the move, the object will have the same shape and size but may be facing a different direction. *See turn.*

rounding: Replacing a number with a number that tells about how much or how many to the nearest ten, hundred, thousand, and so on. Example: 52 rounded to the nearest 10 is 50.

rule: A procedure; a prescribed method; a way of describing the relationship between two sets of numbers. Example: In the following data, the rule is to add 3:

Input	Output
3	6
5	8
9	12

ruler: A straight-edged instrument used for measuring the lengths of objects. A ruler usually measures smaller units of length, such as inches or centimeters.

scale: The numbers that show the units used on a graph.

scale model: A model or drawing based on a ratio of the dimensions for the model and the actual object it represents.

sequence: A set of numbers arranged in a special order or pattern.

Glossary

set: A group made up of numbers, figures, or parts.

side: A line segment connected to other segments to form the boundary of a polygon.

← side

similar: A description for figures that are the same shape, but might not be the same size or in the same position.

slide (translation): The change in the position of a figure that moves up, down, or sideways. Example: scooting a book on a table.

solids: Figures in three dimensions.

solve: To find the solution to an equation or problem; finding the values of unknown variables that will make a true mathematical statement.

sphere: A solid figure in the shape of a ball. Example: a basketball is a sphere.

square: A rectangle with congruent (equal) sides. *See rectangle.*

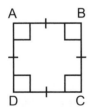

square number: The product of a number multiplied by itself. Example: 49 is a square number (7 x 7 = 49).

square unit: The square with sides 1 unit long used to measure area.

squiggle: *See break.*

standard form: A way to write a number showing only its digits. Example: 2,389.

standard units of measure: Units of measure commonly used; generally classified in the U.S. as the customary system or the metric system:

> **Customary System:**
>   **Length**
>   1 foot (ft) = 12 inches (in)
>   1 yard (yd) = 3 feet or 36 inches
>   1 mile (mi) = 1,760 yards or 5,280 feet
>
>   **Weight**
>   16 ounces (oz) = 1 pound (lb)
>   2,000 pounds = 1 ton (t)
>
>   **Capacity**
>   1 pint (pt) = 2 cups (c)
>   1 quart (qt) = 2 pints
>   1 gallon (gal) = 4 quarts
>
>   **Temperature**
>   degrees Fahrenheit (°F)

> **Metric System:**
>   **Length**
>   1 centimeter (cm) = 10 millimeters (mm)
>   1 decimeter (dm) = 10 centimeters
>   1 meter (m) = 100 centimeters
>   1 kilometer (km) = 1,000 meters
>
>   **Weight**
>   1,000 milligrams (mg) = 1 gram (g)
>   1,000 grams (g) = 1 kilogram (kg)
>
>   **Capacity**
>   1 liter (l) = 1,000 milliliters (ml)
>
>   **Temperature**
>   degrees Celsius (°C)

stem-and-leaf plot: A type of graph that depicts data by occurrence using commonalities in place value. The digit in the tens place is used as the stem. The digit in the ones place is used as the leaf.

straight angle: An angle with a measure of 180°; this is also a straight line.

strategy: A plan used in problem solving, such as looking for a pattern, drawing a diagram, working backward, etc.

Glossary

subtraction: The operation that finds the difference between two numbers.

sum: The answer when adding two or more addends: addend + addend = sum.

summary: A series of statements containing evidence, facts, and/or procedures that support a result.

survey: A way to collect data by asking a certain number of people the same question and recording their answers.

symmetry: A figure has symmetry if it can be folded along a line so that both parts match exactly.

table: A method of displaying data about a topic into rows and columns.

temperature: A measure of hot or cold in degrees.

transformation: An operation on a geometric figure by which another image is created. Common transformations include reflections (flips), translations (slides), rotations (turns), dilations, and contractions.

translation: A change in the position of a figure that moves it up, down, or sideways. *See slide.*

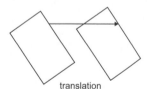

translation

tree diagram: A visual diagram of all the possible outcomes for a certain event. A tree diagram is used to show the probability of a certain event happening.

trend line: A line on a graph that indicates a statistical trend, or tendency of a set of data to move in a certain direction.

triangle: A polygon with three sides. The sum of the angles of a triangle is always equal to 180º.

turn (rotation): The change in the position of a figure that moves it around a point. Example: The hands of a clock turn around the center of the clock in a clockwise direction.

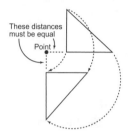

These distances must be equal
Point

unlikely event: An event that probably will not happen.

unorganized data: Randomly presented data that is not presented in a meaningful way.

variable: A symbol used to represent a quantity that is unknown, that changes, or that can have different values. Example: in 5n, the n is a variable.

vertex: The point where two rays meet to form an angle or where the sides of a polygon meet or the point where 3 or more edges meet in a solid figure.

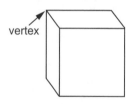

vertex

vertices: The plural of vertex.

volume: The amount of area taken up by a three-dimensional object. The units of measurement used to express volume can be cubic units, such as cubic feet or cubic centimeters, or when measuring fluids, units such as gallons or liters. Volume is usually abbreviated as V and is also called capacity.

weight: A measurement of the amount of force by gravity on a object.

whole number: An integer in the set {0, 1, 2, 3 . . .}. In other words, a whole number is any number used when counting in addition to zero.

Glossary

word forms: The number written in words. Examples: 546 is "five hundred forty-six." The "<" symbol means "is less than." The ">" symbol means "is greater than." The "=" symbol means "equals" or "is equal to."

x-axis: One of two intersecting straight (number) lines that determine a coordinate system in a plane; typically the horizontal axis.

y-axis: One of two intersecting straight (number) lines that determine a coordinate system in a plane; typically the vertical axis.

Examples of Common Two-Dimensional Shapes

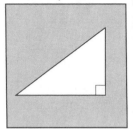

Right Triangle

Isosceles Triangle

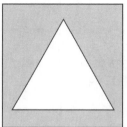

Equilateral Triangle

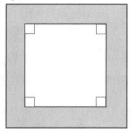

Square

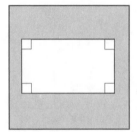

Rectangle

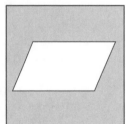

Parallelogram

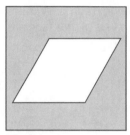

Rhombus

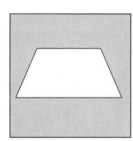

Trapezoid

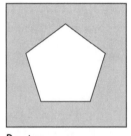

Pentagon

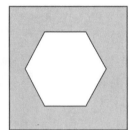

Hexagon

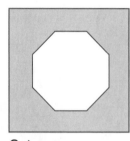

Octagon

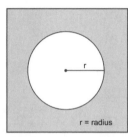

Circle

Examples of Common Three-Dimensional Shapes

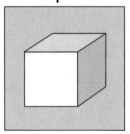

Cube

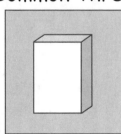

Rectangular Prism

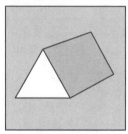

Triangular Prism

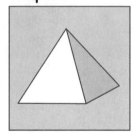

Pyramid

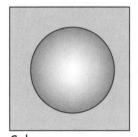

Sphere

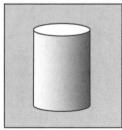

Cylinder

Cone

Examples of How Lines Interact

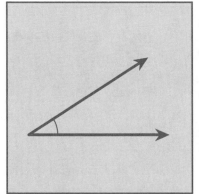

Acute Angle

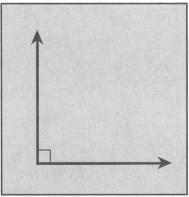

Right Angle

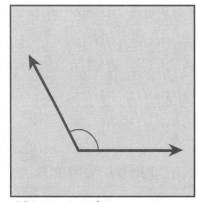

Obtuse Angle

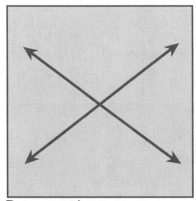

Intersecting

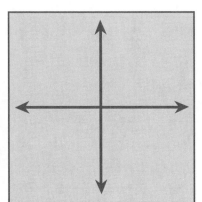

Perpendicular

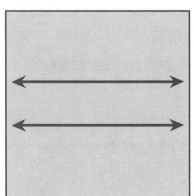

Parallel

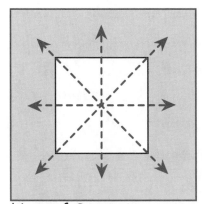

Lines of Symmetry

Examples of Types of Graphs

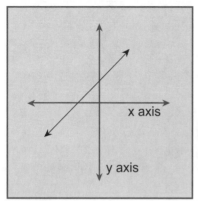

Line Graph

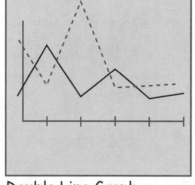

Double Line Graph

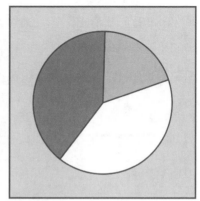

Pie Chart

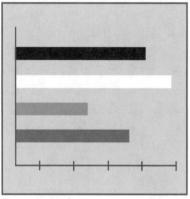

Bar Graph

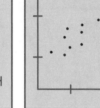

Scatterplot

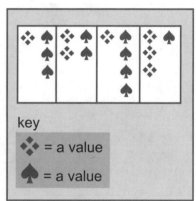

Pictograph

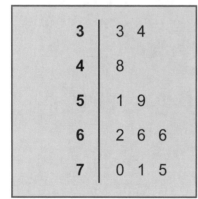

Stem and Leaf Plot

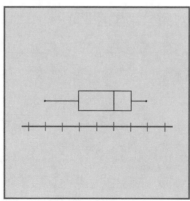

Box and Whisker

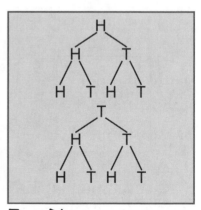

Tree Diagram

Examples of Object Movement

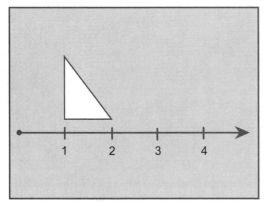 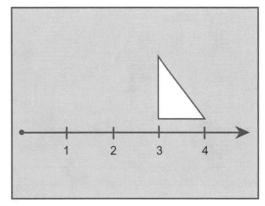

Translation

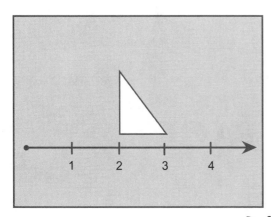 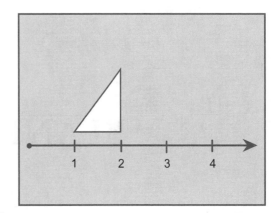

Reflection

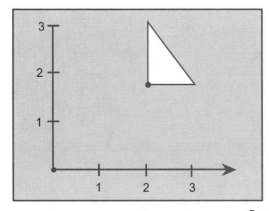 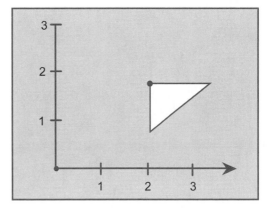

Rotation

BLANK PAGE

Mathematics Practice Tutorial

Directions for Taking the Mathematics Practice Tutorial

The Mathematics Practice Tutorial contains 29 practice questions. You will mark your answers in this workbook. It should take about 30–45 minutes to answer all the questions. If you don't understand a question, just ask your teacher to explain it to you. Calculators and rulers are NOT to be used on the Mathematics Practice Tutorial.

This section will review the Strands, Standards, and Benchmarks used to assess student achievement in the state of Florida. Review these items to increase your familiarity with FCAT-style multiple-choice items. Once you have completed this Tutorial section, you will be ready to complete the Mathematics Assessment.

Sample Multiple-Choice Item

To help you understand how to answer the test questions, look at the sample test question below. It is included to show you what a multiple-choice question in the test is like and how to mark your answer in your workbook.

1 Ronda has 5 stamps. Craig has 30 stamps. Which operation should be used in the box below to find how many stamps Ronda and Craig have combined?

$$5 \boxed{?} \; 30 =$$

● addition

Ⓑ division

Ⓒ multiplication

Ⓓ subtraction

For this sample question, the correct answer is Choice A "addition"; therefore, the circle next to Choice A is filled in.

Mathematics Practice Tutorial

1 The total land area of Florida is fifty-eight thousand, five hundred sixty square miles. How would you write this number?

   (A)   5,856 square miles

   (B)   58,056 square miles

   (C)   58,060 square miles

   (D)   58,560 square miles

2 The chart below shows the finishing times for students who ran the 50-yard dash on field day.

Name	Time
Caroline	7.53 seconds
Carlos	7.09 seconds
Kate	7.5 seconds
Xavier	8.02 seconds

In what order did the students finish the race?

   (F)   Carlos, Kate, Caroline, Xavier

   (G)   Kate, Caroline, Carlos, Xavier

   (H)   Xavier, Caroline, Kate, Carlos

   (I)   Caroline, Kate, Xavier, Carlos

3 William's basketball team is having a pizza party after the game. There are eight players on the team, and three large pizzas with eight pieces each have been ordered. Each player will get an equal amount of pizza. Which picture **best** represents how much pizza each player will get?

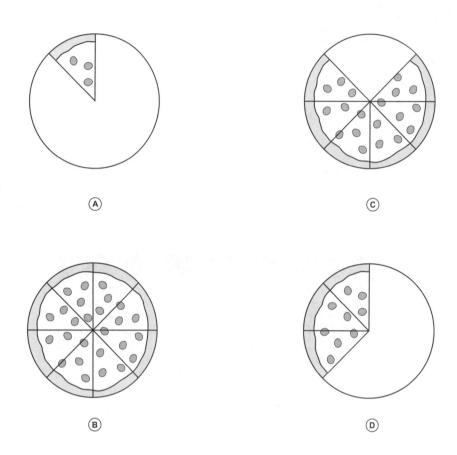

Ⓐ

Ⓒ

Ⓑ

Ⓓ

4 Ursula opened her sock drawer and saw she had a total of 15 pairs of socks in her drawer. Of the 15 pairs of socks she had, 5 of them were blue, meaning $\frac{5}{15}$ of her socks were blue. Which of the following fractions is **equal** to $\frac{5}{15}$?

    (F) $\frac{1}{5}$

    (G) $\frac{1}{3}$

    (H) $\frac{3}{5}$

    (I) $\frac{1}{10}$

5 The highest point in the United States is Mt. McKinley in Alaska. Mt. McKinley has a height of 20,320 feet. In the number 20,320, what place value is the number 3 in?

    (A)   tens place

    (B)   hundreds place

    (C)   thousands place

    (D)   ten thousands place

6 On Monday, the total attendance at Highland Elementary School was 613 students. A total of 627 students go to the school. Which operation should the principal use to find how many students were absent on Monday?

    (F)   subtraction

    (G)   addition

    (H)   division

    (I)   multiplication

Go On ▶

7 On a recent fishing trip, the Summers family caught 25 fish. If each of the 5 members of the family caught an equal number of fish, which of the following could be used to find the number of fish each member of the family caught?

Ⓐ 25 + 5

Ⓑ 25 − 5

Ⓒ 25 x 5

Ⓓ 25 ÷ 5

8 Dan ran 43 miles last week and 51 miles this week. How many **more** miles did Dan run this week?

Ⓕ 8 miles

Ⓖ 11 miles

Ⓗ 12 miles

Ⓘ 94 miles

Copying is Prohibited

9 Look at the chart below. Mr. Oonagi's class took a field trip to a local berry farm. The farmer told the class each berry was used for making something depending on the size of the berry.

Use	Berry Size
juice	0–2 ounces
jam	2–4 ounces
preserves	4–5 ounces
canning	5+ ounces

If the farmer wants to make jam, which berry size should he use?

Ⓐ   1 ounce

Ⓑ   3 ounces

Ⓒ   4.5 ounces

Ⓓ   6 ounces

10 Shari and eleven of her neighbors are playing a game. They want each team to have an equal number of players. Which choice would NOT be a way they could break up into teams?

Ⓕ   3 teams of 4

Ⓖ   2 teams of 5

Ⓗ   4 teams of 3

Ⓘ   6 teams of 2

11 Max plans on putting a fence around his garden which is shown below.

6 meters

Max's Garden

5 meters

What is the perimeter of the garden?

Ⓐ   16 meters

Ⓑ   22 meters

Ⓒ   23 meters

Ⓓ   30 meters

12 On the balance scale below, two striped marbles are needed to equal one silver marble.

If one striped marble weighs 2 ounces, how many ounces does a silver marble weigh?

(F)   1 ounce

(G)   2 ounces

(H)   3 ounces

(I)   4 ounces

13 Which unit of measurement would you **most likely** find on the ruler pictured below?

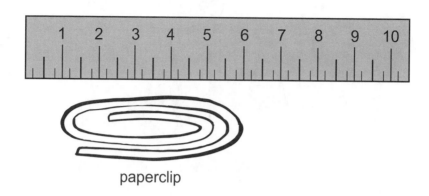

paperclip

Ⓐ   yards

Ⓑ   miles

Ⓒ   centimeters

Ⓓ   liters

Go On

14 Cherries cost $3.88 per pound at the market. Marco bought $8.00 worth of cherries.

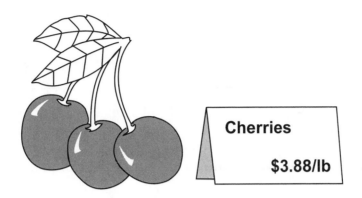

Cherries

$3.88/lb

About how many pounds of cherries did he buy?

Ⓕ   1 pound

Ⓖ   2 pounds

Ⓗ   3 pounds

Ⓘ   4 pounds

15 Marta is traveling by train to visit her friend Valerie. While she is on the train, she is curious to know how fast the train is moving.

Marta's Town   Valerie's Town

Which unit of measurement would the conductor of the train use to tell her the speed of the train?

Ⓐ   miles per hour

Ⓑ   feet per hour

Ⓒ   miles per feet

Ⓓ   miles per second

Copying is Prohibited   © Englefield & Associates, Inc.

16 At the grocery store Kristen used a _____ to find the weight of her fruit.

Which type of instrument should go in the blank?

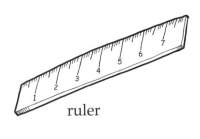

ruler

Ⓕ

measuring cup

Ⓗ

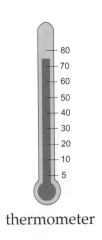

thermometer

Ⓖ

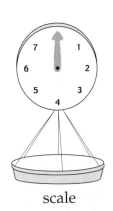

scale

Ⓘ

Go On ▶

17 Which of the following does NOT describe the figure below?

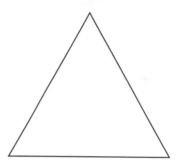

Ⓐ   The figure is a polygon.

Ⓑ   The figure is made up of line segments.

Ⓒ   The figure has three sides.

Ⓓ   The figure contains a right angle.

18 Which pair of shapes is congruent?

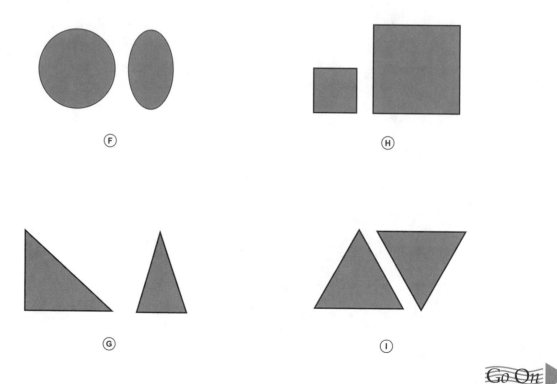

Go On ▶

19 Look at the apple below.

Which apple below shows the apple above turned 180°?

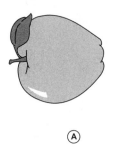

Ⓐ

Ⓒ

Ⓑ

Ⓓ

Go On ▶

20 Pam is going to get carpet in her bedroom. Her room measures 13 feet by 10 feet.

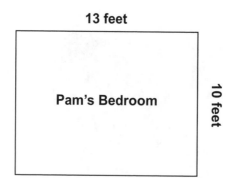

13 feet

Pam's Bedroom

10 feet

How many square feet of carpet will Pam have to buy?

F   130 square feet

G   100 square feet

H   46 square feet

I   23 square feet

21 On the grid below, which point is located at the coordinates (1, 5)?

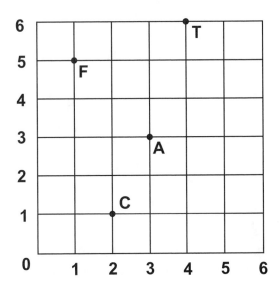

Ⓐ   Point A

Ⓑ   Point C

Ⓒ   Point F

Ⓓ   Point T

22 Which number comes next in the pattern below?

$$3, 6, 9, 12, \text{_____}$$

Ⓕ   15

Ⓖ   16

Ⓗ   17

Ⓘ   18

23 Nicole is 6 years old. Nicole's sister Shawna is 5 years older. Which number sentence **best** represents Shawna's age?

Ⓐ $6 + 5 = \square$

Ⓑ $\square + 5 = 6$

Ⓒ $6 \times 5 = \square$

Ⓓ $\square \times 5 = 6$

24 Coach Jones has 24 team jerseys for the soccer team. There are 8 players on the team. Which number sentence shows the number of jerseys each player will receive?

Ⓕ $24 \div 8 = 3$

Ⓖ $8 \times 3 = 24$

Ⓗ $24 + 8 = 32$

Ⓘ $24 - 8 = 16$

Copying is Prohibited   © Englefield & Associates, Inc.

25 Steve and his friends were having a juggling competition. The graph below represents the number of balls each of them was able to juggle at one time.

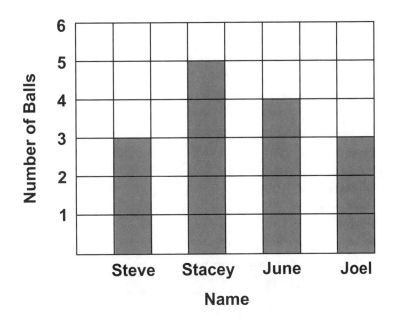

Who was able to juggle the **most** balls at one time?

Ⓐ   Steve

Ⓑ   Stacey

Ⓒ   June

Ⓓ   Joel

26 The shoe sizes of the five members of Yolanda's family are 4, 6, 6, 8, and 9. What is the **range** of the shoe sizes in Yolanda's family?

(F) 4

(G) 5

(H) 6

(I) 7

27 Mario and his friends were catching lightning bugs in jars. Using the chart below, what is the **mode** of the number of lightning bugs caught?

Name	Bugs Caught
Mario	4
Percy	2
Quentin	5
Evelyn	3
Mary	3
Eleanor	6

(A) 2

(B) 3

(C) 4

(D) 6

© Englefield & Associates, Inc.

28 Augie has 5 toy trucks he likes to play with. He is only allowed to play with 2 of the trucks at a time. One of the trucks is red, 1 of the trucks is yellow, and 3 of the trucks are white.

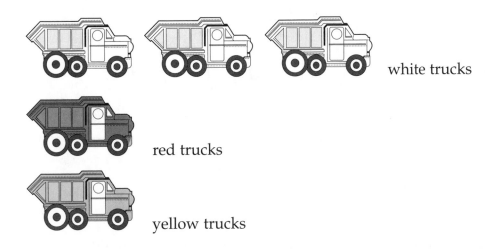

white trucks

red trucks

yellow trucks

How many **different** pairs of trucks would have at least 1 red truck?

(F)   10 pairs

(G)   5 pairs

(H)   4 pairs

(I)   3 pairs

29 Eduardo and his friends are playing the card game Old Maid. Eduardo's cards are pictured below. It is Allison's turn to draw a card from Eduardo.

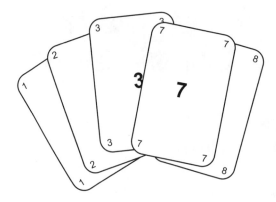

Which statement is **true** about the number on the card Allison will draw from him?

Ⓐ   The "8" is most likely to be drawn from Eduardo's hand because it is on the inside.

Ⓑ   The "2" is most likely to be drawn from Eduardo's hand because it is on the outside.

Ⓒ   The "3" is most likely to be drawn from Eduardo's hand because it is sticking up.

Ⓓ   Each number has an equal chance of being drawn.

This is the end of the Mathematics Practice Tutorial.

Until time is called, go back and check your work or answer questions you did not complete. When you have finished, close your workbook.

BLANK PAGE

Mathematics Assessment

Directions for Taking the Mathematics Assessment

This Assessment test contains 45 multiple-choice questions. Multiple-choice questions require you to pick the best answer out of four possible choices. Only one answer is correct. Remember to read the questions and the answer choices carefully. You will mark your answers in this workbook. Fill in the answer bubble to mark your selection. If you do not know an answer, you may skip the question and come back to it later.

Calculators and rulers are NOT to be used on the Mathematics Assessment.

Mathematics Assessment

1 On their way home from their vacation in Wilmington, North Carolina, Anna and her family saw the road sign shown below.

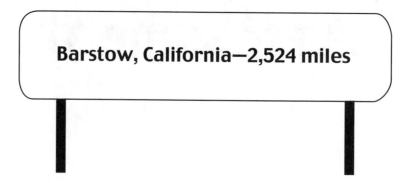

Barstow, California—2,524 miles

How would this distance be written in word form?

Ⓐ   twenty-five thousand twenty-four

Ⓑ   two hundred fifty-two and four tenths

Ⓒ   two thousand five hundred forty-two

Ⓓ   two thousand five hundred twenty-four

2 Marco's brother Ferdinand has a cold. His temperature should be 98 degrees Fahrenheit. What type of instrument should Marco use to check Ferdinand's temperature?

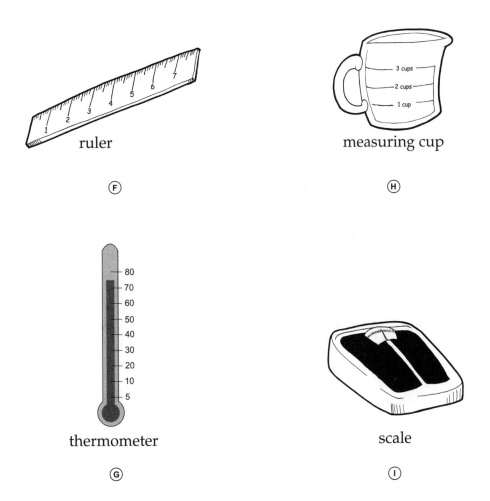

ruler

Ⓕ

measuring cup

Ⓗ

thermometer

Ⓖ

scale

Ⓘ

3 Drew is choosing a snack to have after school. He is allowed to have 1 cookie and a glass of juice. In the cookie jar, he finds 1 chocolate chip cookie and 1 oatmeal cookie. In the refrigerator, he sees 1 bottle of orange juice and 1 carton of apple juice.

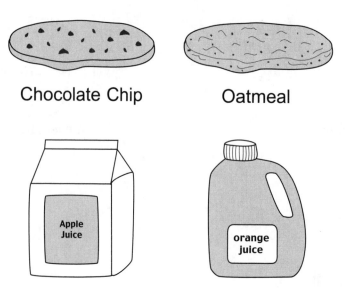

Chocolate Chip　　　　　Oatmeal

How many **different** cookie and juice combinations does Drew have to choose from?

Ⓐ　2

Ⓑ　4

Ⓒ　6

Ⓓ　8

4 Yoshi and his friends went miniature golfing. Their scores on Hole 7 were 1, 4, 2, 2, and 3. What was the **range** of the miniature golf scores?

Ⓕ　1

Ⓖ　2

Ⓗ　3

Ⓘ　4

5   The Children's Museum has a fountain in the main hall.

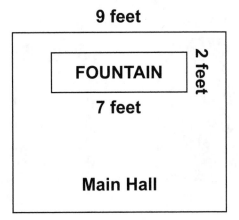

What is the **area** of the fountain in the picture above?

(A)   14 square feet

(B)   18 square feet

(C)   36 square feet

(D)   81 square feet

6 Randy and Lavon each have a jar of candy.

Randy's jar   Lavon's jar

100 pieces   ?

If Randy's jar has 100 pieces of candy, about how many pieces of candy are in Lavon's jar?

- ⒡ 50 pieces
- ⒢ 100 pieces
- ⒣ 200 pieces
- ⒤ 500 pieces

7 Jana started a pet walking service for the summer. She walked 2 pets the first week, 4 pets the second week, and 6 pets the third week. If her business continues to increase at the same rate each week, how many pets will she be walking next week?

- Ⓐ 6 pets
- Ⓑ 8 pets
- Ⓒ 10 pets
- Ⓓ 12 pets

8 Phil is building a new patio. The patio will be 5 meters long and 4 meters wide.

5 meters

Phil's Patio

4 meters

What will the **area** of the new patio be?

Ⓕ   9 square meters

Ⓖ   18 square meters

Ⓗ   20 square meters

Ⓘ   25 square meters

9 What fraction of the rectangle below is shaded?

Ⓐ $\frac{1}{4}$

Ⓑ $\frac{1}{2}$

Ⓒ $\frac{4}{5}$

Ⓓ $\frac{1}{8}$

10 Which of the following **best** describes the figure pictured below?

Ⓕ triangle

Ⓖ parallelogram

Ⓗ pentagon

Ⓘ square

11 Dusty and Meredith are playing Shape Mania. To play the game, they use the spinner shown below.

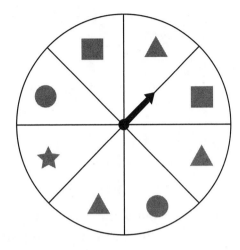

What shape would Dusty or Meredith be **most likely** to spin?

Ⓐ   star

Ⓑ   square

Ⓒ   triangle

Ⓓ   circle

12 The blue whale is believed to be the largest animal ever to have lived. It is the length of three school buses. A blue whale can weigh between 110–150 _____.

What unit of measurement **best** completes the sentence above?

Ⓕ   ounces

Ⓖ   tons

Ⓗ   pounds

Ⓘ   feet

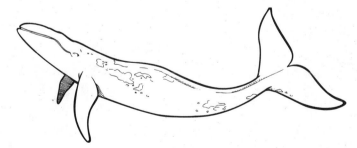

Go On ▶

13 Zack sketched 3 pictures a day for 5 days on his drawing pad. Which number sentence shows the **correct** way to find the total number of pictures Zack sketched over 5 days?

Ⓐ $3 + 5$

Ⓑ 3×5

Ⓒ $5 - 3$

Ⓓ $5 \div 3$

14 The 3 children in the Smith family must wash all the windows in their house. There are 18 windows. Mrs. Smith wants each child to wash an equal number of windows. How will the family decide how many windows each child will wash?

Ⓕ $18 + 3 = 21$

Ⓖ $18 - 3 = 15$

Ⓗ $18 \times 3 = 54$

Ⓘ $18 \div 3 = 6$

Go On ▶

15 On the grid below, where is Point N located?

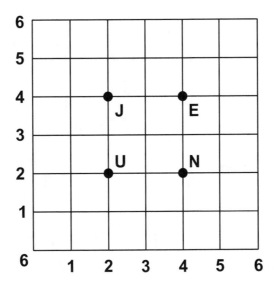

Ⓐ   (2, 4)

Ⓑ   (2, 2)

Ⓒ   (4, 4)

Ⓓ   (4, 2)

16 Which answer choice lists the following numbers from **least** to **greatest**?

10,923   109,230   230,910   93,201   32,091

Ⓕ   10,923; 32,091; 93,201; 109,230; 230,910

Ⓖ   10,923; 109,230; 230,910; 32,091; 93,201

Ⓗ   230,910; 109,230; 93,201; 32,091; 10,923

Ⓘ   10,923; 32,091; 93,201; 230,910; 109,230

Go On ▶

17 On the island of Imaginaria, money value is based on the length of the money. The longer the money, the more it is worth. The Imaginarian money pictured below is worth $1.00.

Which picture is worth $2.00?

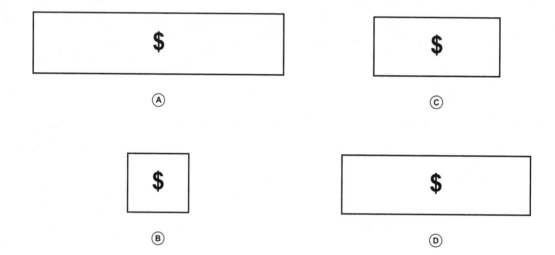

18 Look at the smiley face pictured below.

What would the smiley face look like if it were turned 180° clockwise?

Ⓕ

Ⓗ

Ⓖ

Ⓘ

Go On ▶

19 Read the following statements in order to find the Mystery Number.

Mystery Number Clues:
1. One of my factors is 4.
2. I am between 10 and 20.
3. One of my factors is 8.

What is the Mystery Number?

Ⓐ   12

Ⓑ   16

Ⓒ   18

Ⓓ   24

20 The students in Mr. Sefton's class took a survey to see what holiday was most popular with the students in their class. They put their results into the graph below.

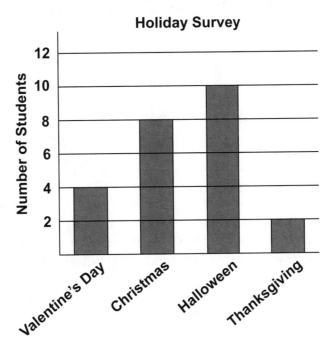

Holiday Survey

How many students are in Mr. Sefton's class?

(F)   10 students

(G)   12 students

(H)   24 students

(I)   28 students

21 The Everglades cover 1,507,850 square miles of Florida. In the number 1,507,850, which number is in the hundreds place?

(A)   0

(B)   5

(C)   7

(D)   8

Go On

22 Mrs. Chen's class took a field trip to the zoo. She has 27 students in her class. When they arrived at the zoo, they divided into two groups. Group A had 12 students in it. If the rest of the students were in Group B, how many students were in Group B?

- Ⓕ 12 students

- Ⓖ 13 students

- Ⓗ 14 students

- Ⓘ 15 students

23 Jill took her favorite glass from home to school to use in a science experiment. She wanted to find how much water her glass held. Which unit of measure will Jill's answer be in?

- Ⓐ feet

- Ⓑ ounces

- Ⓒ gallons

- Ⓓ grams

24 Rahul's mother gave him $\frac{1}{2}$ of $1.00 to take to the movies to buy a snack. How much money did Rahul have for a snack?

- Ⓕ $0.12

- Ⓖ $0.20

- Ⓗ $0.50

- Ⓘ $0.66

Copying is Prohibited
© Englefield & Associates, Inc.

25 Juniper and Andrea each bought a baseball. Each bought her baseball at a different store. Juniper's baseball cost $5.00. Andrea's baseball cost $3.00. Which equation could be used to find how much **more** Juniper paid for her baseball?

Ⓐ $5 - 3 = \square$

Ⓑ $5 + 3 = \square$

Ⓒ $5 \times \square = 3$

Ⓓ $5 \div 3 = \square$

26 Carrie likes to do puzzles. She can do a 200-piece puzzle in 50 minutes.

If she starts a new 200-piece puzzle at 1:00 p.m., at **about** what time will she finish the puzzle?

Ⓕ   1:30 p.m.

Ⓖ   2:00 p.m.

Ⓗ   2:30 p.m.

Ⓘ   3:00 p.m.

27 Rosaria went to the pet store to buy a new fish for her fish tank. When she got to the store, she saw there were 5 tanks with 6 fish each. Which operation should she use to find the **total** number of fish in the fish tanks?

Ⓐ   addition

Ⓑ   subtraction

Ⓒ   multiplication

Ⓓ   division

28 On field day, the third-grade class held a water balloon-throwing contest. The chart below shows the number of water balloons each player was able to catch in a row.

Name	Balloons Caught in a Row
Carter	3
Paul	1
Randall	0
Nicki	2
Stacy	3
Janelle	3

What is the **mode** of the number of water balloons the players were able to catch in a row?

Ⓕ   3

Ⓖ   2

Ⓗ   1

Ⓘ   0

29 Which figure is congruent to the figure pictured below?

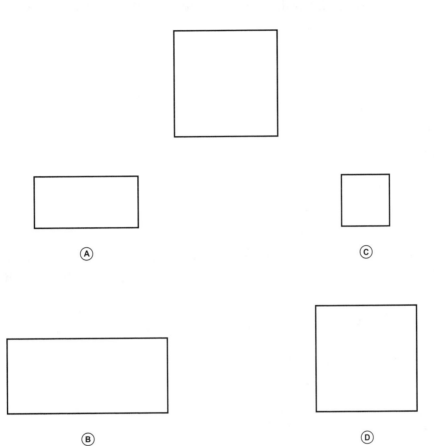

Ⓐ

Ⓒ

Ⓑ

Ⓓ

30 Read the following statements in order to find the Mystery Number.

Mystery Number Clues:
1. I have 4 digits.
2. My tens digit is greater than my ones digit.
3. I have a 7 in the hundreds place.
4. My thousands digit is less than my hundreds digit.

What is the Mystery Number?

Ⓕ   3,621

Ⓖ   4,712

Ⓗ   471

Ⓘ   4,721

31 The Atlantic Coast of Florida has 399 miles of shoreline and the Gulf Coast has 798 miles of shoreline. How many **more** miles of shoreline does the Gulf Coast have than the Atlantic Coast?

Ⓐ 399 miles

Ⓑ 401 miles

Ⓒ 798 miles

Ⓓ 1,197 miles

32 Kim collected 19 shells while walking on the beach for 10 minutes. If she continues collecting shells at this rate, about how many shells will she be able to collect in 30 minutes?

Ⓕ 30 shells

Ⓖ 40 shells

Ⓗ 50 shells

Ⓘ 60 shells

Copying is Prohibited   © Englefield & Associates, Inc.

33 On the graph below, which point is located at (2, 3)?

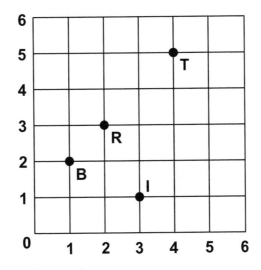

(A)   Point B

(B)   Point I

(C)   Point R

(D)   Point T

34 Oscar was outside collecting ladybugs. He caught 6 ladybugs total. He counted the spots on each ladybug and found the ladybugs had the following number of spots: 6, 7, 3, 8, 4, and 4. What is the **range** of the number of spots on the 6 ladybugs?

(F)   3

(G)   4

(H)   5

(I)   6

35 Mr. Duncan is a farmer. He has two chickens that he collects eggs from. On one day, one of the chickens laid 8 eggs and the other chicken laid 6 eggs. Which number sentence represents the **total** number of eggs laid by the two chickens?

Ⓐ $8 + \square = 6$

Ⓑ $6 + \square = 8$

Ⓒ $6 + 8 = \square$

Ⓓ $6 \times 8 = \square$

36 The length of the equator is about 24,902 miles. What number is in the tens place in the number 24,902?

Ⓕ   0

Ⓖ   2

Ⓗ   4

Ⓘ   9

37 When Allison was getting ready for school one morning, she noticed she only had 3 pairs of socks in her sock drawer. One pair of socks was white, one pair was red, and the other pair was blue.

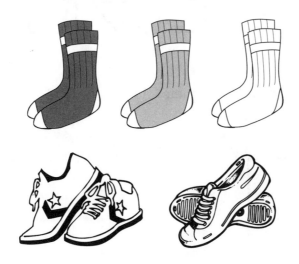

If Allison has 2 pairs of tennis shoes to pick from, how many **different** combinations of pairs of socks and pairs of tennis shoes does Allison have to choose from?

Ⓐ 4

Ⓑ 5

Ⓒ 6

Ⓓ 8

38 Cindi designed the pattern shown below to put on her bicycle.

Which shape should go next to complete Cindi's pattern?

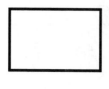

Ⓕ

Ⓗ

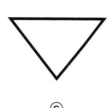

Ⓖ

Ⓘ

Copying is Prohibited
© Englefield & Associates, Inc.

39 Which unit of measurement would be used to measure the amount of water a swimming pool holds?

    (A)   grams

    (B)   gallons

    (C)   pounds

    (D)   meters

40 Which shape is NOT a polygon?

    (F)   triangle

    (G)   square

    (H)   circle

    (I)   hexagon

41 Rob had 12 seeds and 3 pots to put them into. He put the same number of seeds into each pot.

Which number sentence shows how to find the number of seeds he put into each pot?

Ⓐ   12 ÷ 3

Ⓑ   12 x 3

Ⓒ   12 + 3

Ⓓ   12 − 3

Go On ▶

Copying is Prohibited   © Englefield & Associates, Inc.

42 Which of the following shows a line of symmetry on the picture?

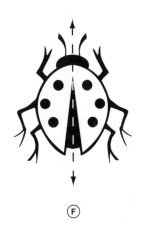

Ⓕ

Ⓗ

Ⓖ

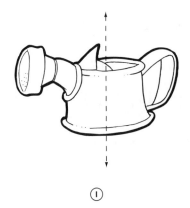

Ⓘ

Go On ▶

43 Jessie is moving to a new house. She wants to find out if her couch will fit through the front door. Which unit of measurement should be used to measure the height of a door and the length of the couch?

Ⓐ mile

Ⓑ foot

Ⓒ millimeter

Ⓓ kilometer

44 Hector had $9.00. His grandmother gave him money for his birthday, and then he had $14.00 altogether. Which number sentence **best** represents how much money Hector's grandmother gave him?

Ⓕ $14.00 + $9.00 = ☐

Ⓖ ☐ ÷ $14.00 = $9.00

Ⓗ $14.00 − $9.00 = ☐

Ⓘ ☐ x $9.00 = $14.00

Go On ▶

45 Look at the tally table below.

Favorite After-School Activities	
Watching TV	IIII
Playing video games	ⅣHL II
Riding bikes	ⅣHL II
Playing with pets	II
Playing sports	ⅣHL IIII

According to Luis' tally table, what is the **mode** of Luis' set of data?

Ⓐ 2

Ⓑ 5

Ⓒ 7

Ⓓ 9

This is the end of the Mathematics Assessment.
Until time is called, go back and check your work or answer questions you did
not complete. When you have finished, close your workbook.

Notes

Notes

Notes

Notes

Show What You Know® on the 3rd Grade FCAT
Additional Products

Show What You Know® on the 3rd Grade FCAT, Parent/Teacher Edition

Flash Cards for Reading and Mathematics

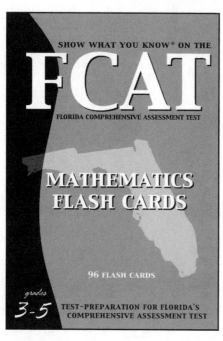

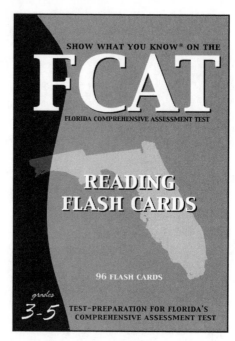